The Way I See It

Other books by the author

Face Up with a Miracle
Handbook on Holy Spirit Baptism
Spiritual Power: How to Get It and How to Give It
Deliver Us from Evil
True and False Prophets
The Miracle of Tongues
The Most Dangerous Game
Manual for Spiritual Warfare
Lead Us Not Into Temptation

The Way I See It

Don Basham

Fleming H. Revell Company
Old Tappan, New Jersey

Scripture quotations, unless otherwise indicated, are from THE HOLY
BIBLE: NEW INTERNATIONAL VERSION (North American Edition).
Copyright © 1973, 1978, 1984, by the International Bible Society. Used by
permission of Zondervan Bible Publishers.
Additional translations used are:
New American Standard Bible, copyright © The Lockman Foundation 1960,
1962, 1963, 1968, 1971, 1972, 1973, 1975, 1977.
Quotations marked KJV are from the King James Version.

Library of Congress Cataloging in Publication Data
Basham, Don, 1926–
    The way I see it.

"A Chosen book."
    1. Meditations.   I. Title.
BV4832.2.B333   1987   242   86-26227
ISBN 0-8007-9098-7

A Chosen Book
Copyright © 1986 by Don W. Basham
Chosen Books are published by
Fleming H. Revell Company
Old Tappan, New Jersey
Printed in the United States of America

To Alice,
whose constant love and encouragement
are intricately woven into everything I write;
and to our children,
Cindi, Shari, Glenn, Lisa, and Laura,
and their families—
further living proof of our effective collaboration—
this book is affectionately dedicated.

Contents

– Introduction

For most of us, life consists of a few extraordinary days joined together by many ordinary years. Between rare mountainpeak experiences, we live in valleys of the commonplace and on plains of the ordinary.

I believe one of the great challenges of the Christian life is learning how to find spiritual significance in everyday things. "Who despises the day of small things?" Scripture asks (Zechariah 4:10). Too many of us, I'm afraid.

We need to understand that God is not only the God of great things; He is the God of little things. He who spoke the universe into existence notes the fall of every sparrow and numbers the hairs on our heads. He is not only the God of history, He is God over all our daily events. To press home this truth, Jesus drew most of His parables from common, everyday situations. He said, "The kingdom of heaven is like . . ." and then spoke about a woman losing a coin, a farmer sowing seed, a shepherd seeking a lost sheep, a man inviting guests to a wedding, servants working in a vineyard, a father instructing his sons . . . all situations with which ordinary people could identify.

So often we long for some earthshaking spiritual event to miraculously catapult us out of our ordinary circumstances—when what we may really need is more grace to see God at work in our daily affairs.

Upon hearing the sighs of a believer distressed over the unending parade of daily frustrations, a patronizing Christian friend declared, "We are called of God to share the Gospel to a dying world; we shouldn't let little things distract us."

Such observations sound so noble and righteous that sincere believers tend to feel guilty when they hear them. Yet no matter how devoted to God we are and how noble our Christian aims, we must still deal with life's frustrations one day at a time. "Do not worry about tomorrow," Jesus said. "Each day has enough trouble of its own" (Matthew 6:34). It's great to want to win the world, but first we have to make it through the day. And idealistic pronouncements about the nobility of Christian service really don't help much.

I remember hearing a veteran missionary who had been inspired by such sentiments describe his disillusionment on arriving overseas to begin his first term. Filled with anticipation and excitement, he entered the small furnished living quarters he was to share with an experienced older missionary, only to find all the furniture moved to one side of the apartment with a chalk line drawn along the center of the floor.

Surrounded by furniture his co-worker said, "This half of the house is mine!" Then pointing defiantly at the empty half, he said, "You live over there."

"I thought I was called to preach the love of God to the heathen," the missionary reflected. "But first I had to find daily grace for living with an embittered servant of God."

One day years ago God whispered to me, "Look for Me in little things." That's what I've tried to do in these essays. While some might be called sermonettes, most of them reflect simple experiences in life—looking out my office window, riding on a jet plane, playing with my grandchildren, watching waterfowl in the sky, hunting and fishing with my father, taking flying lessons, some happy and some not-so-happy childhood experiences, seminary days, buying a new car, various preaching experiences. The stories contain no great revelations, no earthshaking pronouncements—mostly they are just reflections about everyday living, with some insights that may help you get through the day.

Some years ago I went through a barren period, when trying to write anything creative or inspiring seemed to take Herculean effort. I had experienced no great tragedy or crisis, but day-by-day coping with life became extremely difficult. During that time when even prayer and Bible reading were hard, I found comfort in short inspirational articles and essays in magazines like *Reader's Digest* and *Guideposts*. Those pieces often helped to lift my gloom, at least momentarily. And they helped assure me that everyone endures such low periods at one time or another. In short, they helped lighten the load of the day.

For many years I had written regularly for *New Wine* magazine. So, as I recovered from my slump, I asked the editorial board for permission to include a new short feature in our magazine, a monthly page reflecting on some simple truth or spiritual insight. Since *New Wine* provided primarily Bible-teaching articles designed to help Christians grow spiritually, a monthly page of philosophical musings was something of a calculated risk. Nevertheless, the editorial board graciously granted its permission.

The encouraging response to "The Way I See It" indicated the page found special favor with many *New Wine* readers. In fact, it was a reader of *New Wine,* also an editor for Chosen Books, who first encouraged me to submit a collection of such essays for a possible book.

While some essays included here have not been previously published, many have appeared on "The Way I See It" page in

New Wine magazine. I wish to thank the publishers of *New Wine* for their gracious permission to reprint them here.

For most of us, even the smallest encouragement is welcome if it will help to lift us above the frustrations and pains of the daily grind. When asked what proved the greatest trial of his thousand-mile trek across an African desert, a famous explorer replied, "The sand in my shoes."

I pray these essays may help remove some of the sand from your shoes.

Don W. Basham
P.O. Box 1720
Elyria, Ohio 44036

The Way I See It

— 1

The Harrowed Sparrow

What can a man learn by sitting in his office staring out the window? You might be surprised. Over a year ago, *New Wine* magazine moved into new offices located on lovely, wooded property. I have a corner office with large windows facing north and east. The windows are mirrored glass; I can see out but no one can see in.

One morning I was delighted to see two bobwhite quail appear on the top of a terrace wall just outside the east window. I stood close to the glass and for several minutes watched the lovely wild birds peacefully sunning and preening themselves. Had I tried to approach them from the outside, I couldn't have come within a hundred yards. But with the mirror-window between us, I stood unnoticed, only an arm's length away.

God, are You watching me, as I am watching them? I wondered.

In His teachings, Jesus sometimes indicated we could learn from the birds.

"Look at the birds of the air; they do not sow or reap or store away in barns, and yet your heavenly Father feeds them. Are you not much more valuable than they?"

Matthew 6:26

"So don't be afraid; you are worth more than many spar-
rows."   Matthew 10:31

But even birds, who have no real worries, are not always
peaceful and trusting. A few mornings after watching the quail, I
heard a thump at the east window and looked up from my work
to see a slightly dazed mockingbird pick himself up off the win-
dowsill and dive at the window again, pecking furiously at his
own reflection in the glass. All morning long, that silly, angry
bird kept scratching and pecking at what he thought was a rival
or an enemy. The next morning he was at it again, and the next.

I could have helped that bird had he been able to hear me. I
could have told him that if he would just stop fighting and turn
away, the "enemy" would also turn away from him. Then he
could go on building his nest in peace. But tapping and shouting
from my side of the glass did no good at all.

God, are You watching me, as I am watching him? I wondered.

I suddenly realized how frustrated God must feel when we
turn from trusting Him to go knocking our heads against some
perceived "threat" to our welfare—a threat that in reality may
be only the reflection of our own angry initiative.

After some days, the mockingbird disappeared. I thought he
had learned his lesson until one morning when I met with
Charles Simpson in his office on the other side of the building.
There was that stubborn mockingbird, banging his beak against
Charles' window. He hadn't learned a thing; he had only changed
windows.

As long as we trust Him, the Lord will provide for us just as
He does for the birds who "do not sow or reap or store away in
barns." But He will not stop us if we decide to forsake that trust
temporarily, to go knocking our heads against the reflection of
our own fears and suspicions, anymore than He stopped that
stubborn mockingbird.

So if you are currently engaged in pecking away at some fearful, deceiving reflection, the answer may be to repent, turn your back on it, and get on with trusting and serving God.

Changing windows is no help at all.

Keep Watch!

Twenty-five years ago I was pastor of a liberal denominational church in Toronto, Canada. It was a complacent congregation whose primary spiritual conviction seemed to be that a weekly one-hour worship service with a fifteen-minute sermon should provide quite enough religion for any normal person. But as a young Bible-believing minister, I stubbornly attempted to deepen that conviction by preaching regularly on great scriptural truths that most of the congregation considered irrelevant.

One Sunday morning I preached an eloquent and inspiring sermon on the Second Coming of Christ. At least, between the time I finished preparing the sermon on Friday and rose to preach on Sunday, *I* believed it would be eloquent and inspiring. But when I started to preach, the words seemed to dribble off my chin and hit the floor six inches in front of the pulpit. I felt like a fool. Instead of awesome inspiration, my sermon produced only amused toleration in the congregation. Which, in turn, produced great exasperation in me.

Monday morning as I sat fuming in my church study, the seventy-year-old associate minister entered, shaking his gray head and smiling.

"Where did you ever find the courage to preach *that* message to *this* congregation?" he asked.

Naturally, I was defensive. "It's an important subject and I thought it would help encourage the congregation. But apparently no one believed a word I said."

"Don't take it so hard, Don." The associate pastor meant to be helpful. "Few people listen to sermons anymore and fewer yet believe in Christ's Second Coming."

Today, Bible critics and skeptics are still quick to point out that the New Testament writers' hope for Jesus' early return went unfulfilled, and that Paul was wrong when he spoke about those "who are still alive, who are left till the coming of the Lord" (1 Thessalonians 4:15).

But were the disciples mistaken to look for the Lord's return? Is it so foolish for us to believe in the Second Coming? Not if we take the words of Jesus seriously. "Therefore keep watch," He said, "because you do not know on what day your Lord will come" (Matthew 24:42).

Keep watch! That means, be expectant! Knowing the specific day of His coming isn't crucial, but our attitude about His coming is.

Keep watch! We look for the Lord's return, not to escape our trials or excuse our failures, but as the thrilling climax to all we've worked for and believed in.

Keep watch! We look for the Lord's return, not because He will snatch us from the claws of the antichrist, but because He is coming to reign in person over the Kingdom for which even now we labor.

Keep watch! No one knows the day or hour, but it could be today!

Keep watch! For the coming of the One "whose certain return at an uncertain time has been the hope of the Church through the ages."

So even I, and with a pang more thrilling,
So even I, and with a hope more sweet,
Yearn for the sign, O Christ, of thy fulfilling,
Faint for the flaming of thine advent feet.[1]

No, the New Testament writers weren't wrong to look for the Lord's return, and neither are we. They lived their days surrounded by the certainty of His coming, no matter the exact hour or day. Their expectancy—and ours as well—is a constant reminder of a victory already won, of the ultimate triumph of God's purpose in the earth.

[1] F. W. H. Myers, *St. Paul.* London: MacMillan Co., Ltd., 1867.

3

That's How It Is
with Intercessors

To be an intercessor for others is one of the unique privileges we have as Christians. In spiritual warfare, any one of us can become a casualty, stricken and unable to get into the presence of God unless faithful friends bring us before the Lord. The story of one such man who had to rely on his friends to bring him into the presence of God is found in the healing of the paralytic in Mark 2.

The incident took place early in the public ministry of Jesus when great crowds gathered everywhere He went. Some of the people came to see Him out of curiosity, some to receive help, and some simply to find reasons to condemn Him. The crowd that filled the house in Capernaum where Jesus was teaching that day must have contained some of all. But four men came with yet another motive. Carrying a paralyzed friend, they had one purpose in mind: to get their friend into the presence of Jesus so he could be healed.

Getting into God's presence is not always easy. Sometimes we have to overcome strong resistance; sometimes it takes perseverance and painful, sacrificial effort. This was such a time. Not only

could the four men not get close to Jesus, they couldn't even get
near the door! Lesser men might have given up, but love for
their brother filled the four with desperate determination. They
headed for the roof.

Imagine the scene. The room is packed with people listening
to Jesus preach when loud noises begin to break out above them.
Suddenly dirt and debris from the ceiling shower down on their
heads, and on the Lord's head as well. They shield their eyes
with their hands and squint up at the ceiling—or what used to be
the ceiling. For now, great portions of the roof have been ripped
away, allowing the sunlight to stream down into the room.
Through the large gaping hole four anxious faces peer down.

Imagine the indignation of the crowd, the hisses of disapproval
from the scribes, the dismay and anger of the homeowner! Who
are these ruffians? How dare they wreck the house and interrupt
the meeting! And what's that they're lowering through the hole
in the roof?

The crowd looked up through the haze and dirt and debris and
saw rudeness; they saw lack of respect; they saw deliberate de-
struction of property. But that's not what Jesus saw. He looked
up through the same haze of dirt and debris and saw faith—the
desperate, loving faith of men who were willing to endure whatever condemnation might follow their reckless act. He saw faith
in eight scratched and dirty hands gently lowering the pallet with
its pitiful load until it rested directly in front of Him.

Immediately the Lord responded to that faith. The Scripture
here is magnificently understated: "When Jesus saw *their faith*,
he said to the paralytic, 'Son, your sins are forgiven. I tell you,
get up, take your mat and go home'" (Mark 2:5, 11, italics
added).

To the astonishment of everyone except Jesus and the four
friends on the roof, the paralytic jumped to his feet, folded his
mat under his arm, and made his way out of the room in perfect
health.

It is interesting to note that Jesus never spoke to the men on the roof, nor did the healed paralytic pause to look up and thank them as he headed for home a whole man. There was no public acknowledgment, no public praise for them. But I suspect that failing to receive recognition never fazed the four men. They were too busy rejoicing and too filled with gratitude for what the Lord had done for their friend.

That's usually the way it is when you become an intercessor, for intercessors aren't public figures and intercession is not a public ministry. People may never know the part you play in helping a miracle happen. But you know, and you know that God knows—and that should be quite enough.

4

The Danger of
Throwing Rocks

The Bible is as relevant today as when it was written, not simply because it is the Word of God, but because human nature doesn't change. Apart from God's grace, people today have the same tendency toward evil they've had since Eve gave Adam the apple, even if outward techniques are more refined.

Long before His crucifixion, Jesus' enemies tried to do away with Him by pushing Him over a cliff and by stoning Him (see Luke 4:28–29 and John 10:31–32). Today pushing people over cliffs and crucifixion are in poor taste, but stoning is very much in vogue. Of course, not literal stones that kill the body, but verbal stones that assassinate character—stones of gossip, criticism, and condemnation.

In John 8:2–11, when self-righteous scribes and Pharisees brought the woman caught in adultery (but not the man!), insisting she be stoned, Jesus said two things. To the Jews He gave a firm rebuke: "If any one of you is without sin, let him be the first to throw a stone at her" (verse 7). Then, to the woman, He spoke forgiveness and encouragement: ". . . Neither do I condemn you. Go now and leave your life of sin" (verse 11).

In the Sermon on the Mount, Jesus said, "For in the same way you judge others, you will be judged, and with the measure you use, it will be measured to you" (Matthew 7:2). Jesus obviously understood human nature. The louder we condemn or criticize the faults of others, the more likely it is that we have committed—or at least have secretly longed to commit—the same sin.

In Luke 15, the elder brother of the prodigal complained bitterly to his father about the royal welcome the penitent son received.

> "But when this son of yours *who has squandered your property with prostitutes* comes home, you kill the fattened calf for him!"   verse 30, italics added

Actually, the elder brother had no direct knowledge of how the prodigal had squandered his inheritance. His complaint was simply a confession of what he would have done had he been bold enough to claim his inheritance and leave town the way his brother did. Inwardly, he was as much a prodigal as his younger brother, only without the daring.

The elder brother's attitude reminds me of an incident that happened years ago when a prominent church in the city where I also pastored suffered a minor scandal. The minister was caught in a questionable situation with a woman parishioner. Though there was the appearance of impropriety, no actual immorality occurred.

Nevertheless, the ruling elder in the church, a man of great wealth and national prominence, condemned the pastor in thunderous tones and the church board fired him. Some months later the whole city was shocked when it was discovered that the self-righteous elder had fathered an illegitimate child by a mistress he was seeing at the very time he condemned his own pastor.

Jesus knows full well the weaknesses of human nature. That's why He insists that we not judge one another. As the old couplet says,

> There's so much good in the worst of us,
> And so much bad in the best of us,
> It scarcely behooves any of us
> To talk about the rest of us.

We can all say *Amen!* to that.

5

Banquet Tables and Battlegrounds

Thou preparest a table before me in the presence of mine enemies.
Psalm 23:5, KJV

A striking picture hangs on our dining room wall, a photograph depicting a magnificent banquet table with lovely place settings arranged on a beautiful white tablecloth. The location is out of doors at twilight, the table extending into the distance as if it were endless. The caption beneath the picture reads, "Come, for everything is now ready" (Luke 14:17), a verse from Jesus' parable of the great banquet. In Luke 13:29 the banquet is referred to as "the feast in the Kingdom of God" and in Revelation 19:9 as the "wedding supper of the Lamb."

But in the parable in Luke 14, so many of those invited began to make excuses that the host became angry and opened the banquet to the poor and lame and crippled off the streets. The parable's implication is clear: many who think they have it made will miss the wedding supper, while the poor and needy will enjoy its blessings.

How tragic that today so many whom the Lord invites to His banquet table still refuse to come, and even more tragic are their lame excuses! In the parable, one claimed he had to examine a real estate purchase. Another said he had to check five newly purchased teams of oxen. Still another excused himself as a new-lywed! Today, the excuses would be "I'm watching television" or "I have to catch a plane" or "That's my bowling night!" But are those who ignore the Lord's invitation today in any less danger than those about whom Jesus spoke?

While I trust that no one reading this essay will miss out on the marriage supper of the Lamb, the truth is, many of us do miss certain blessings the Lord would have us enjoy, simply because we fail to understand both the ways of God and the nature of spiritual warfare.

When I look at that lovely picture on my dining room wall, I think not only of the marriage supper of the Lamb, but of other opportunities for feasting and fellowshiping with the Lord I have missed.

In the past we have not normally associated banquet tables with battlegrounds, but it's time we began. The key to what I'm suggesting lies in one startling phrase found in the middle of Psalm 23. I sometimes wonder: Out of all the millions of Christians who have faithfully prayed the Twenty-third Psalm, how many have actually paused to ponder the meaning of that one startling phrase?

"Thou preparest a table before me *in the presence of mine enemies*" (verse 5, KJV, italics added).

We long for green pastures and still waters. We are thankful for His presence in shadowed valleys, and for the comfort of His rod and staff. We praise him for the anointing and the overflowing cup and rejoice in His everlasting goodness and mercy.

And we want to rejoice in His bounty, in the banquet tables He spreads for us. But how about the location of that particular banquet table? It's not in the safety of a church fellowship hall, nor the shelter of a Holiday Inn or Sheraton! No, sometimes His table for us is spread in the presence of our enemies. Not fifty miles behind the lines, but right on the battlefield!

Shall we examine the implications of the location of that banquet table? It says something about the unceasing nature of spiritual warfare. It says something about the attitude God wants us to have toward those we war against. It says that we are not to fear them nor to be intimidated by them, that we can trust Him to protect us from their attacks while we fellowship and dine with Him.

Few of us believe that a major source of God's goodness and mercy could be a banquet table spread for us in the presence of our enemies. But as spiritual warfare increases, there may be less and less opportunity to feast with the Lord at tables spread anywhere else.

By faith, we must learn to claim the peace, the power, and the provision of God, right where the battle is raging, even while the enemy is taking aim. If that seems an unusual idea, remember these are unusual times. They are not times meant for hiding from the enemy nor for waiting for the war to end.

No matter where the banquet table is located, let us be eager to join Him there. Who knows what we may miss if we allow the strange location of the banquet table to deter us from enjoying the rich blessings of His banquet!

6

A Special Gift

When I was growing up in Texas, I spent some of my happiest days hunting ducks and geese with my father and brothers. It wasn't the hunt so much as the wild beauty of those flights of waterfowl that thrilled me. I knew most species of waterfowl by name: surface-feeding ducks like mallard, pintail, teal, and widgeon; deep-water diving ducks like the canvasback, blue bill, redhead, and goldeneye. Then there were Canada geese, brant, snow geese, and white-fronted geese.

Even today I consider a flight of wild geese stretched in graceful formation against an autumn sky to be one of the loveliest sights on earth. For me, the annual pilgrimage of waterfowl south in autumn and north in spring testifies not only to the beauty of God's creation but to its timeless order and harmony as well.

Though I was a Christian by the age of nine, I'm afraid I found more of God in the sunrises and sunsets on calm Texas prairies and in the splendid flights of ducks and geese than I found fidgeting on the pews of our family's church. Those precious outdoor days became a significant part of my heritage, reminders that God is not only my Redeemer but a special friend with whom I continue to share a special love.

A specific reminder of that heritage occurred one day last fall when my wife, Alice, and I drove along the shore of the Gulf of Mexico, not far from where we then lived in Mobile, Alabama. Even though cottages and condominiums lined most of the shoreline, we passed one open stretch of beach where sea gulls wheeled in the sky as fingers of sunlight sifted through broken clouds, streaking the surface of the water with silver. Suddenly in the midst of that tranquil scene, a formation of four wild geese— wings set for landing—came sliding down the sky, passing just above our car.

"Those are geese!" I cried. "And they're going to land!"

I slammed on the brakes and made a quick U-turn. At first, we couldn't see where they had landed; then there they were—four majestic white-fronted geese, standing on the grassy lawn separating a line of three-story condominiums from the highway. I pulled to the side of the road with a sense of awe. Wild geese just don't normally sail down four-lane highways and land on condominium lawns, at least not in Alabama.

The geese, I figured, began their migration from Alaska or northern Canada weeks before, headed for their final destination in southern Mexico or Central America. How had their arrival at this particular spot on the Gulf of Mexico managed to coincide exactly with ours? And what prompted them to land so close to the road? As I pondered their selection of such an unusual landing spot, I could almost see God smiling.

For another ten minutes we watched the geese as they rested on the grass fewer than a hundred feet away. They seemed to be studying us as well. Then I put the car in gear to pull away. The geese also seemed to know our visit was over, for at the same moment they lifted into the air and turned toward the Gulf. Clearing the roof of the condominium, they rose higher over the beach, disappearing into the southern sky.

"Thank You, Lord," I said, and turned our car toward home.

Some people may ask, "Why would God go to all the trouble of arranging something like that just for you and Alice?" I don't know; I just believe He did. And I don't really think it caused Him any trouble, either. Rather, I believe God delights in giving such gifts—precious tokens of His love beyond our asking. Only we're often too blind or busy to see them.

Our unexpected visit with the four wild geese lasted only a brief fifteen minutes, but gratitude to the One who arranged it will warm my heart for a lifetime. Some days bring special gifts from God.

7

High Flight

One evening, my two-year-old grandson, Toby, and I watched a movie about old World War I airplanes. Toby was so excited he began to run around the room imitating the sound of the airplane engines.

"Z-a-r-o-o-m, Papa!" he shouted, glancing at me. "Z-a-r-o-o-m!"

Just like his grandfather, I thought.

Ever since I was Toby's age, I've been fascinated with airplanes. As a boy, I used to make model airplanes and on weekends would beg my father to drive me out to the Wichita Falls airport to watch the planes take off and land.

Our family was on vacation in Washington, D.C., when finally, at age twelve, I first got to fly. My father paid a charter pilot $7.50 to take my two brothers and me for a fifteen-minute ride over the Capitol city in a four-place 1933 Stinson. As I looked down on the capitol building, the Lincoln Memorial, and the Washington Monument, I hadn't the slightest inkling that some twenty years later, I would be pastoring a church in that very city.

In 1943, at the age of sixteen, I graduated from high school and went to work in a local war plant. Intrigued as ever by air-

planes and now having a steady income, I received my parents'
permission to take flying lessons.

My training plane was a little yellow Piper Cub, which had a
cruising speed of 60 miles per hour and a landing speed of 38
miles per hour. After several hours of dual instruction, I was allowed to solo. As any pilot will testify, no other thrill quite
matches that first solo flight—the long-awaited day when your
instructor crawls out of the airplane, and you take off alone.

Most of my flying time after I soloed, I spent either practicing
landings on the grass runway or meandering lazily two thousand
feet above the flat Texas prairies and wheat fields. But one summer day I decided to see how high the little yellow Cub would
fly.

I took off into a blazing blue sky that was half filled with cu-
mulus clouds. At six thousand feet I passed the base of the
clouds, and a few hundred feet higher what had begun as a simple joy-ride became a spiritual pilgrimage. Wandering among
giant white columns billowing upward, towering like worshiping
sentinels along the boundaries of some vast cathedral in the sky, I
felt as if God had granted me special permission to explore a part
of His creation most men would never see. For a glorious, intox-
icating forty-five minutes I steered my tiny craft up and down
halls of splendor, and when finally, reluctantly, I returned to
earth, a part of me never quite made it down.

It's hard to describe that experience; I'm not sure I ever tried
until now. But God gave another young pilot, a poet, such inspiration that his words give perfect expression to the silent testimony of my own heart.

High Flight
Oh, I have slipped the surly bonds of earth,
And danced the skies on laughter-silvered wings,
Sunward I've climbed and joined the tumbling mirth
Of sun-split clouds—and done a thousand things—

You have not dreamed of—wheeled and soared
  and swung.
High in the sunlit silence, hov'ring there,
I've chased the shouting wind along and flung
My eager craft through footless halls of air.
Up, up the long delirious burning blue,
I've topped the wind-swept heights with easy grace,
Where never lark, or even eagle flew;
And while with silent lifting mind I've trod
The untrespassed sanctity of space,
Put out my hand and touched the face of God.

I was seventeen years old when I first found a copy of that poem and placed it in my wallet. I was just two years younger than its author, John Gillispie Magee, was when he wrote it. Magee, the son of a Congregational minister, joined the Royal Canadian Air Force in 1939 and became a fighter pilot. Shortly after he composed *High Flight*, he was killed in aerial combat over the English Channel. He was nineteen years old.

Despite the years that have passed since I first read Magee's poem, every time I read it or hear it still (the United States Air Force has used it in its recruiting commercials on television), it touches me as deeply as the first time.

Nowadays, giant jets ferry thousands routinely through the clouds every day, and no one pays much attention. But I still do. Every time I board one of those jets and we climb toward heaven, I inevitably relive that summer afternoon in 1944 when I first prayed with the clouds and felt some secret door in my spirit swing open toward God.

8

More Than I Deserve

I don't find it hard to believe that God loves me; only that He *always* loves me—even when I'm rebellious or disobedient. One Scripture that clearly confirms that He does is the story of the Prodigal Son in Luke 15. Having ended up in a foreign pigsty, the prodigal repents and heads for home. Then verse 20 says,

> "But while he was still a long way off, his father saw him and was filled with compassion for him; he ran to his son, threw his arms around him and kissed him."

The father's compassionate welcome means so much to me because of my own battle through my years as a Christian to fully accept that nothing I do—no matter how foolish or stupid—diminishes God's love for me or alters the truth that I am His child. Like any small child, I struggle to comprehend father-love.

"Daddy, do you really love me?"

"Yes, son, I love you."

"Do you love me all the time?"

"Yes, son, I really do—all the time."

"Even when I'm bad, Daddy? Do you love me even when I'm bad?"

"Yes, son, I love you even when you're bad."

I remember one incident that made me very aware of the reality of a father's love. I was seven years old and it was a hot summer afternoon when someone shouted the challenge.

"Let's go play in the Bashams' yard. Last one across the street's a rotten egg!"

Instantly, nine neighborhood children, ages six to thirteen, bolted into the street, oblivious of oncoming traffic. In fifth place and intent on overtaking the boy ahead of me, I didn't see the car or hear the squeal of its brakes until it was too late. I was struck from behind and slammed face down on the pavement, the car sliding to a stop directly over my body, one front wheel inches from my head. Stunned and terrified, I crawled slowly and painfully from under the car. Ignoring the anguished face of the driver as he jumped from his car, I limped into the front yard of my own home. As my father and mother rushed out the door and down the steps toward me, I finally found breath enough for one long, agonizing wail.

Moments later, I was standing in the kitchen shaking like a leaf, my father behind me with protective hands on my shoulders, my mother on her knees in front of me, using a damp cloth to gently sponge the dirt and blood from my skinned face, elbows, and knees. I was shaking not only from the shock of being struck and almost killed by the car, but also from the awful weight of my own disobedience. How many times had my parents warned, "Look both ways before you cross the street!"

I finally cried, "Mother, Daddy, I'm so sorry! Are you going to spank me?" only to be lifted suddenly into the fierce but tender embrace of my father and to feel my mother's tearful kisses cover my face. Until that day when foolish disobedience almost cost me my life, I never really knew how much my parents loved me.

On more than one occasion over the years since then I have found that same boundless, unconditional love, only in far greater measure, in my relationship with my heavenly Father. For sometimes, temporarily deviating from His will, I have rushed headlong into selfish, worldly traffic only to be knocked flat by some powerful temptation I should have seen coming. Then, hurt and humiliated, I have come to my senses and turned limping in repentance back to the Father's house, only to be overwhelmed by the unfailing grace that rushed to embrace me.

The miracle is not just that God loves us, but that He seems to love us most when we are the least deserving.

9

I May Have Been Wrong About That

Last week I watched a television program in which a prominent philosopher was interviewed by a highly literate journalist. At one point the philosopher took several minutes to explain why he had come to hold a particular conviction. As I listened to the brilliant articulation of his position, I wondered how anyone could disagree with him.

But then the journalist gave a contrasting point of view based on a different set of philosophical ideas. I sat forward in my chair, waiting for the defense I felt would surely follow—that stern, authoritative kind of response that learned men are prone to make when challenged.

But it didn't come. The philosopher listened thoughtfully to the journalist's arguments. "Yes, I see the point you are making," he said. "I never considered that before. Of course, I have always believed . . ." and he restated his own thesis in a few sentences. Then, with a smile, he added, *"But I may have been wrong about that."*

I don't remember the issue in question, but I will never forget the gracious concession of that philosopher. "I may have been wrong about that." What rare words!

How long has it been since you heard a politician make such an admission? Or a preacher? Or an employer? Or a parent? Or—for that matter—yourself? Yet how much better life would be if we were secure enough in God to make such an admission when the situation called for it.

Spoken at the right time and place, that simple phrase could have changed the course of history. Suppose when Adam was confronted by God for eating the forbidden fruit, instead of blaming Eve, he had said, "I may have been wrong about that."

Or suppose when the Jews heard the truth from Jesus, instead of plotting to kill Him, they had confessed their hypocrisy and said, "We may have been wrong about that."

Convictions are important, of course, and we all share some basic beliefs that provide motivation for faithful Christian living. But we also cling to certain mistaken, self-serving views that not only blind us to truth and wisdom God has given others, but often goad us into imposing our own will on others in a manner that makes them suffer.

We need to remember that in every disagreement and in every strained or broken relationship there is fault on both sides. Who's most at fault usually doesn't matter. What counts is the willingness to humble ourselves and say, "I may have been wrong about that."

Before the Civil War, General Robert E. Lee commanded the West Point Military Academy. A story is told about two of his senior staff officers who had a violent disagreement. Lee summoned the men to his office. The orders he gave to end the argument contained the wisdom of Solomon. He said, "The one who is least at fault will be the first to apologize."

If we could only realize that such a gracious admission does not diminish us in the sight of others; rather it raises their opinion of us. It is not a sign of weakness; it is a sign of wisdom. It does not reflect past prejudices so much as present openness.

"I may have been wrong about that" can be a healing, reconciling, bridge-building statement that clears the way for all sorts of wonderful, redemptive events to take place.

Who knows? Perhaps some of you reading this are ready to make just such an admission, ready to forsake some old prejudice still masquerading as strong conviction. There was a time when as a zealous and impatient young minister, I was certain other people couldn't change and even more certain that I shouldn't change. But many times through the years I have come to see that I was wrong, both about them and myself.

Moreover, I suspect I still hold certain prejudices I label as convictions about which one day God will show me it is time to say, "I may have been wrong about that."

10

"You Said You'd Carry Me!"

Sometimes with the very best of intentions we try to do more for people than is good for them or right for us. In Galatians 6, Paul says we must sometimes "carry each other's burdens" (verse 2), but other times "each one should carry his own load" (verse 5). That means sometimes it's right to help and sometimes it isn't. How, then, can we learn the difference between burdens to be shared and burdens to be carried alone? Well, there's no substitute for experience. . . .

One spring day in Texas when I was a young man, my father and I set out to go fishing. When we stopped at a shallow river near the lake to seine minnows for bait, I discovered I had left my hip boots at home. After some discussion, it was decided we could still seine minnows. I could walk, dry-shod, along the river's edge, pulling my end of the seine, while Dad waded in the river, pulling his.

But between us and the river stretched a slough of stagnant water about eighteen inches deep and fifteen feet across: too wide to jump and too long to walk around. As I recall, it was my father who first proposed the hasty and ill-fated solution to my bootlessness.

"You hold the seine and the minnow buckets, and I'll carry you across on my back," he offered. Good old Dad! Always ready to help!

So I climbed onto his back and Dad, properly clad in his hip boots, stepped carefully into the water. I was 20 years old, 6 feet tall and weighed 200 pounds. Dad was 58 years old, 5 feet 8 inches tall, and weighed 150 pounds. Unfortunately, we failed to take into consideration the crucial effect of weight redistribution. Had each of us crossed the slough alone, the soft bottom would have easily sustained our separate weights, but. . . .

The piggyback ride proceeded smoothly enough at first. Then, halfway across, the bottom turned too soft to support 350 pounds on one pair of legs, and I listened in dismay to my father's chilling appraisal of our situation.

"I'm stuck! You'll have to get off."

All I could think of were my nice dry khaki trousers and my shiny leather shoes, neither of which was designed for water sports.

"What do you mean, get off? I can't get off—I'll get wet!" I grabbed Dad tighter than ever. "You can make it. We're only a few feet from the bank!"

But my father viewed our dilemma from a starkly different perspective.

"I can't go on," he explained patiently. "I'm stuck and I'm about to fall. So I want you to get off my back."

I grabbed him all the tighter. "No! I don't want to get wet— you said you'd carry me!"

But my pointed reference to an earlier commitment fell on deaf ears. Dad's original inspiration had seemed valid at the time, but stuck in the slough with me on his back, he received added insight in the form of two new, shining truths. First, his resources were insufficient to deliver both of us; and second, even a father's love has its limits.

His next words confirmed that our predicament was primarily

my fault and that the cause of justice is most fairly served when only the guilty suffer.

"No sense in both of us getting wet," he said.

One ruthless shrug of his shoulders was all it took. I hit the water in a sitting position, seine and minnow buckets flailing all around, and watched my father calmly proceed to the shore. Then he turned and smiled.

"Son, you look mighty silly just sitting there in the water. Come on, let's go."

"B-but y-you deliberately d-dumped me!" I sputtered my indignation. "My own father!"

Dad turned and headed for the river. "Yes, but you'll dry off. And we still have minnows to seine and fish to catch. Next time you won't forget your boots."

My father was right. I did dry off; we did seine minnows; and we did catch fish. And next time I didn't forget my boots. In fact, I never, ever forgot my hip boots again.

But perhaps the most important lesson I learned that spring day in Texas was that we should be careful not to depend too much on those who are willing to help us, lest our load become too heavy for them. Some burdens we can share, but others we must carry alone.

11

To Believe
or Not Believe

When I was pastoring the church in Toronto, a young house-wife on crutches from a paralyzing disease was miraculously healed in our weekly prayer meeting. Because few people in our congregation believed in miracles, we had quite a stir the following Sunday morning when Lillian walked proudly and gratefully to the front of the church to testify to what God had done for her. Exclamations of surprise and unbelief exploded all around. Some who cried, "I can't believe it!" were overjoyed and rushed to give her a hug. Others who cried, "I can't believe it!" stood aloof and muttered darkly, "She'll be back on crutches tomorrow."

Those responses were expressions of two kinds of unbelief. There is an unbelief that longs to believe—as expressed by those who hugged Lillian—and that rejoices when faith fulfills its promise. But there is also an unbelief that *refuses* to believe, that scornfully rejects even the clearest evidence of God's divine intervention. One kind of unbelief God can use; the other He cannot.

The first kind of unbelief represents the struggle we all have when trying to trust God more than our circumstances. This kind of unbelief is epitomized in Scripture by the father of the epileptic boy described in Mark 9. While Jesus was on the Mount of Transfiguration, the father brought his son to the disciples, who were unable to free him from his torment. When Jesus returned, He said to the father, "If thou canst believe, all things are possible to him that believeth" (Mark 9:23, KJV).

The father's response was totally honest. "I believe; help thou mine unbelief" (verse 24). Although the father's faith was mixed with unbelief, when that imperfect faith made contact with the perfect faith of Jesus, it was sufficient; the boy was set free!

The Bible also tells us about another kind of unbelief that even Jesus could do nothing to change. The last few verses of Matthew 13 describe a heartbreaking visit by Jesus to his hometown. Not only were the people of Nazareth skeptical as He taught in the synogogue, they were actually offended when He began to pray for the sick. "And they took offense at Him. . . . And He did not do many miracles there because of their unbelief" (Matthew 13:57–58, NAS).

The people in Jesus' hometown didn't just suffer from ordinary unbelief; theirs was a scornful unbelief—a calculated, unbelieving unbelief. Because of that unbelief, the people of Nazareth deliberately turned their backs on the Son of God and forfeited the grace that could have been theirs.

We should be encouraged to realize, however, that God doesn't require a great faith or a perfect faith for wonderful things to happen. The father of the epileptic boy had only a tiny faith, no larger than a mustard seed (see Matthew 17:19–20). And by the father's own admission, his tiny faith was mixed with an unbelief that longed to believe. Nevertheless, when it was joined to the perfect faith of Jesus, it wrought a miracle.

If we can only believe it, that's the way it can be with us. We needn't despair that our tiny mustard-seed faith is still linked to an unbelief, *as long as it is an unbelief that longs to believe,* for once it is joined to the perfect faith of Jesus, all kinds of miraculous things are suddenly within our reach.

— 12

Praying It In

Recently, while on a plane heading home from a speaking engagement, I found myself reading a small book about George Mueller, known as "the man of faith to whom God gave millions." Best remembered as the founder of the Bristol Orphanages in England, Mueller also established many other ministries, sustaining them all solely through prayer. In his lifetime he "prayed in" an astounding 1½ million pounds sterling, the equivalent in purchasing power to more than fifty million 1986 dollars.

For some sixty years Mueller kept a journal in which he regularly recorded both his needs and God's faithfulness in meeting those needs. Here is part of the journal entry for July 28, 1874, written when he was sixty-nine years of age:

> If it pleases Him to make me do again in the evening of my life what I did from August 1838 to April 11, 1849 . . . gladly will I again pass through all those trials of faith, if He only might be glorified and His Church and the world be benefited.

Then Mueller described his current situation:

> *All funds gone* and 2,100 persons to be totally provided for; *all funds gone* and 189 missionaries to be assisted; *all funds*

gone and 100 schools with 9,000 students to be provided for.

But once again God met those needs as He continued to do until George Mueller's death at age ninety-two. Asked just one year prior to his death if God had always been faithful, Mueller replied, "Always! For nearly seventy years every need in connection with this work has been supplied. Hundreds of times we have commenced the day without a penny, but our Heavenly Father has sent supplies the moment they were actually needed. No man can ever say I asked him for a penny; we have no collectors, no committees, no endowment. All has come in answer to believing prayer."

As I continued reading his testimony on the airplane, I recalled how in 1968 I gathered my wife and children together and in one drastic, exciting step, left the security of a denominational pastorate to begin my own "faith ministry." Just as Mueller had done, Alice and I resolved to ask no man for money; we were fully prepared for a lifetime of "praying it in." For several years we experienced—on a small scale—answers to prayer as dramatic as any given Mueller. Those were awesome, scary, glorious days.

Then after a few years we began to prosper and could say with Paul, "I know what it is to be in need, and I know what it is to have plenty" (Philippians 4:12). Our joy, however, has not been so much in the prosperity itself, as in our awareness that God is the source of it. And each morning I awake knowing that if He asked, we could gladly give it all away and return to praying in our daily provision. Just as we did for several years—just as George Mueller did for seventy years! For it was during such times that Alice and our children and I learned the depth of God's love and the intimacy of His care. Such assurance should be at the heart of every Christian's faith.

George Mueller died March 10, 1897, but today tens of thousands of believers continue to be inspired by his testimony.

Some cautious Christians like to remind us that God doesn't call everyone to live like George Mueller. That may be true. Still, I can't help feeling that multitudes of Christians would be immeasurably strengthened by imbibing a strong dose of George Mueller's faith. The result would be a flood of new, vital testimonies to God's ability and willingness to provide for us. The Church is always in need of those!

— 13

Unlikely Disciples

Have you ever wondered why Jesus didn't choose a more suitable group of men than the original twelve? There was no shortage of trained religious professionals to choose from—priests, scribes, lawyers, Pharisees, and Sadducees—but Jesus bypassed them all for a band of nobodies. Even with the exception of Judas Iscariot, the other eleven seemed singularly unqualified—fishermen, a tax collector. . . .

What's more, the head of the twelve, Simon Peter, seemed the unlikeliest disciple of them all. Arrogant, blustery, unstable, and double-minded, he blew hot and cold. Jesus never knew which direction Peter was coming from! One minute he seemed to soar on heights of revelation, faith, and confidence, the next minute reverting to arrogance, violence, and faithlessness.

In Matthew 14, Peter's impetuous faith produced a miracle that he alone shared with the Lord. While the other disciples clung to the sides of their storm-tossed boat and watched in wonder, Peter "walked on the water to Jesus" (verse 29). And it was Peter's openness and sensitivity to the Holy Spirit that led him to be first to declare, "You are the Christ, the Son of the living God" (Matthew 16:16). Jesus blessed him for his revelation.

Yet only a few verses later, that same Peter arrogantly began to rebuke Jesus for His determination to face the Cross: "Never, Lord! This shall never happen to you!" (verse 22). Imagine having gall enough to rebuke Jesus! Jesus looked Peter in the eye and rebuked the spirit of Satan speaking through him: "Out of my sight, Satan . . ." (verse 23).

Talk about double-mindedness! One minute Peter had been the mouthpiece for the Holy Spirit, proclaiming Jesus as the Christ, the next minute the mouthpiece for Satan, rebuking Jesus in an attempt to turn Him from the purpose of His Father. One minute he was so courageous that he would kill to protect Jesus (see John 18:10–11), but the next minute so filled with fear that he swore three times he never knew the Lord (see Mark 14:66–72).

Yet, amazingly, Jesus never lost confidence in Peter. Beyond Peter's fear and the humiliating denials, He discovered a quality in Peter that was worth saving him for, worth helping him make it through.

"Simon, Simon, Satan has asked to sift you as wheat. But I have prayed for you, Simon, that your faith may not fail. And when you have turned back, strengthen your brothers."   Luke 22:31–32

Jesus' prayer was answered. It was Simon Peter who on the day of Pentecost preached in the power of the Holy Spirit and saw three thousand souls saved.

Peter made it through!

I can identify with Peter. And because Jesus saw Peter through, I believe He'll also see me through. Like Peter, at times I have enough faith to walk on water—to proclaim the Lordship of Christ and to teach and preach with signs following!

But I also know what it is to act and speak as if I never knew the Lord, then taste the bitter tears of repentance. At times, I've been so prideful and arrogant I have rebuked the Lord when I disagreed with His plan and purpose for my life. And sometimes I've been angry enough to slice off the heads of those who seemed opposed to what I wanted to do for God.

But always afterward, with penitent heart and ear, I think I hear the Lord say, "Satan has asked to sift you as wheat, but I have prayed for you, Don, that your faith may not fail. And when you have turned back, strengthen your brothers."

No, Jesus didn't pick extraordinary men to be His disciples. He chose weak, quarrelsome, prideful, fearful men and shared with them His vision of the Kingdom of God. Then He taught them, trained them, and entrusted to them the Gospel, knowing His grace alone would make up the difference.

On that basis I believe I qualify as a disciple, and I suspect that's the only way *you* qualify as well.

14

Out of the Miry Clay

When I was a boy growing up in Texas, our family drove to the Colorado mountains every summer for a week of trout fishing. The summer I was seventeen, I had an experience I have never forgotten.

My father and I were fly-fishing along the edge of a mountain lake. It was late afternoon, and trout were hitting the top of the water everywhere. I was wading into knee-deep water, casting my fly line ahead of me, when suddenly my feet plunged deeply into a soft section of lake bottom. Struggling to lift my foot, I felt my left foot sink deeper into the mire. Trying to lift my left foot sunk me even deeper. Every effort to extricate myself made matters worse.

Cold lake water was soon pouring in over the top of my hip boots as the water level crept steadily toward my waist. Fighting panic, I looked around for something to grab hold of. Nothing was in reach. The solid rocky shore was only ten feet away, but it might as well have been a mile.

I was about to cry for help when a hundred yards down the shoreline I saw my father, who had seen my dilemma, racing toward me. Scarcely breaking his stride, he snatched a long dead tree limb from the water's edge and, reaching the point on shore opposite me, thrust the dripping limb toward me.

"Son, throw your fly rod ashore and grab the limb with both hands!" he instructed. I did as I was told, and moments later I was standing safely on dry ground, soaked to my armpits, covered with mud from the waist down, and minus one boot that had been swallowed by the mire.

Deliverance came because I had a father watching over me who could do for me what I could not do for myself.

In the years since, I have frequently seen that scary experience as a spiritual illustration of many other experiences in life. In difficult situations we are too prone to rely on ourselves rather than trusting God, but struggling in our own strength just seems to get us in deeper.

Scripture often makes the same point. No man served God more faithfully than David, the shepherd king. He had many glorious successes. Yet David was human, and sometimes, as he himself testified, his own sin and mistakes created difficulties too great for human solution. Only God could save him.

He [the Lord] lifted me out of the slimy pit, out of the mud and mire; he set my feet on a rock and gave me a firm place to stand.   Psalm 40:2

My father is in heaven now, and in more than thirty-five years as a minister and Bible teacher, I have spent much more time fishing for men than fishing for trout. Yet during my years of ministry, I have had to experience that same kind of rescue more than once.

Sometimes stubbornly pursuing some individual effort of my own, I fail to watch where my momentum is taking me, and suddenly find myself deeply mired in a complicated, muddy situation I hadn't counted on.

Trying to extricate myself by strictly human effort usually makes matters worse. I find myself sinking deeper, until the shock of cold water pouring over the top of my ministerial boots finally reminds me I need my Father's help.

Perhaps the kind of personal dilemma I've described here is familiar to you as well. Most of us seem to have a real knack for getting ourselves into situations we can't get ourselves out of. So if that's your present problem, remember there is a Father who watches over you and who stands ready to do for you what you cannot do for yourself.

And if you will stop struggling long enough to look farther down the shore, you may see the One who knows you are sinking, and—with deliverance in hand—is racing in your direction.

15

Pedestals Are
for Statues Only

Every man in public ministry collects his own share of "pedestal placers," that is, loyal followers who mentally fashion elaborate pedestals for him. In my case, God periodically arranges for me to fall off every pedestal, thus confirming both to me and the pedestal placers that I am not "God's man of faith and power." I'm just an ordinary Christian who puts his trousers on one leg at a time.

Some years ago I was ministering at a five-day conference in Texas at a time when I had only partially recovered from a severe viral infection. Upon arrival at the conference, I informed the host minister of my problem and asked to be excused from the usual round of personal counseling sessions and after-meeting social gatherings that normally accompany such a conference. He graciously honored my request until the last day of the meeting. Then he asked if I would mind if an "influential" woman in his church joined us for dinner just before the final session.

"She has received so much help from your books she's just dying to meet you," he explained. Then he added, "It will also make things easier for me after you have left town."

Although I was extremely tired, I felt I behaved in a fairly courteous manner during dinner. But as soon as the meal was over, I excused myself and returned to my room for some rest before the meeting.

The next morning as my host drove me to the airport, I thought he seemed unusually quiet. Finally he said, "I must tell you that the woman who joined us for dinner last night was terribly offended by your behavior."

I was stunned. "Whatever did I do to upset her?"

"After you left the table," he explained, "she became furious. She said she had been looking forward to meeting you for months, but then you just sat there and ignored her during the whole meal. She said you weren't anything at all like she imagined from reading your books!"

"But didn't you explain to her that I've been sick?"

"Yes, I did. But she still said she thought you were about the rudest man she had ever met."

The problem, of course, was the pedestal! According to the lofty one she had me on, I should have spent the entire dinner hour entertaining her with scintillating conversation filled with sparkling gems of spiritual wisdom. Sadly, all I could think about was finishing my meal and getting an hour's rest before I had to speak. I feel sure my failure to meet her expectations provided food for some caustic comments to her friends about "what traveling Bible teachers are really like!"

Satan employs a cunning tactic for promoting discord when he tricks us into putting people on pedestals, because the moment they fall off we begin to resent and criticize them.

"Why, I never dreamed that my husband/wife/pastor/employer/neighbor/friend would do a thing like that!" we say. And then we go plowing up the peace and sowing seeds of discord, self-righteously venting our shock and outrage because people we held in high regard have failed to measure up to our impossible expectations.

The truth is, people almost always fall short of our expectations. And much of the time the problem is not so much poor performance on their part as unreasonable expectations on ours.

Even John the Baptist had certain expectations about the kind of ministry Christ would conduct when He came, and Jesus didn't seem to be fulfilling them.

> When John heard in prison what Christ was doing, he sent his disciples to ask him, "Are you the one who was to come, or should we expect someone else?"   Matthew 11:2–3

The devil has a way of enlarging our expectations of others until they sometimes assume proportions that no mortal could possibly fulfill. He prompts us to fashion pedestals of near perfectionism and place those we admire on top of them. Sooner or later—because such pedestals don't allow for human frailty—those we put there come crashing down.

Pedestals aren't meant for real live people; they are meant only for statues. That's because only statues never misbehave. They never fail or fall short of people's expectations. They never complain or become angry or miss appointments. Statues never have bad days. They just stand there on their pedestals, looking important and waiting to be admired.

But for real live people who are placed on them, pedestals are a pain. They are no help at all. They leave no corner for compassion; they have no ledge for love. Pedestals provide no walls for weakness to lean against; they extend no pity for poor performance. Pedestals grant no grace to cover failure and offer no second chances.

We think when we place people on pedestals, they neither need our help to stay there nor deserve our help when they fall. But we are wrong on both counts.

So the next time you decide to place someone on the lofty pedestal of your own unrealistic expectations, do your best to resist the temptation. Not only the person you admire, but the whole Body of Christ will be better off.

— 16

Designed to Fly
Straight and Level

One of the biggest challenges Jesus had with His disciples was to increase their awareness of God in their daily living. One way He sought to do that was by drawing spiritual lessons from all kinds of ordinary things. He spoke of shepherds and sheep, farmers and crops, wells and water, birds of the air, and lilies of the field. If He were teaching on earth today, I believe Jesus would still draw lessons from ordinary things—from television, computers, automobiles, and airplanes.

I know from experience there are spiritual lessons to be learned from airplanes. When as a teenager I learned to fly in the little yellow Piper Cub, it was called the "safest airplane ever built." And not without reason. One lazy summer day when I was practicing precision turns three thousand feet above sunny Texas wheat fields, my instructor explained why the Piper Cub was held in such respect.

"Don," he said to me, "if you ever lose control of this airplane, just turn loose of the stick and take your feet off the rudder pedals. The plane will right itself because *it's designed to fly straight and level.*"

Then he demonstrated what he meant. He put the airplane into a radically steep, climbing turn. Then, just before we lost flying speed, he took both hands and feet off the controls. The little plane immediately nosed down, picked up speed, wallowed a bit before leveling its wings, and then returned to straight and level flying. That little Piper Cub could fly better by itself than most men could make it fly, resting confidently in the air that surrounded and supported it.

I flew that plane for several years. Although I never experienced a crisis such as my instructor described, I never forgot his words or that sturdy little aircraft's serene performance. In the decades since, I have learned how that same quality of inherent stability applies to life in the Kingdom of God. We all endure trials and turbulent times when things seem temporarily out of control, but that in no way nullifies the balancing, stabilizing factor we call the grace of God.

After I received my pilot's license, I had occasion to fly with many other pilots in that same little airplane. Some of those pilots seemed to become a part of the plane the minute they took the controls. For them, flying was sheer joy. But other pilots seemed to fly almost as if the aircraft were an adversary.

From takeoff to landing, they "overcontrolled." They would pump the control stick, kick the rudder pedals, push and pull the throttle, fiddle with the trim tabs, and tap the dials on the instrument panel with their fingertips, as if the airplane could stay aloft only by their keeping both hands and feet in constant motion. For them, flying seemed to be a strain if not an agony.

Through the years I have met scores of Christians like that second group of pilots. Good, earnest believers who have never really learned to trust God, they spend their years pumping, kicking, pushing and pulling, fiddling and tapping. Determined to make the Christian life fly by their own activity and efforts, they miss the sheer joy of the grace of God for fear of falling out of the sky.

I have often wished I could take each of those people up in

that little Piper Cub and show them how it flies straight and level all by itself, confident in its inherent stability and in the unfailing support of the air surrounding it. Perhaps I could help them find some of the peace and stability that is ours in Jesus Christ and help them rest confidently in the grace of God that surrounds and supports them as surely as the air around that little yellow airplane.

Perhaps then they would understand that God has destined us for Kingdom living and that regardless of life's turbulence, we are designed to fly straight and level.

Pleasing Father

We were in the home of our son, Glenn, recently, and I watched with pleasure as he encouraged his son, Michael, who was just learning to walk. It was obvious that no small part of Michael's motivation to succeed was the delight it brought his father. He would take a few wobbly steps before hitting the floor, and immediately Glenn was there to scoop him up in his arms, hug him, and encourage him to try again.

It doesn't seem all that long since I was encouraging Glenn to take his own first faltering steps, and I can easily recall early times with my own father when I was learning to run. I remember the thrill of racing across the grass, the wind in my face, with the loving figure of my father hovering alongside, saying, "Faster, son! Run faster!"

An even greater thrill came when I was sixteen and my father took me on my first deer hunt. The day started miserably as I missed a big buck that jumped up right in front of me. He disappeared into the brush before I could get a second shot.

At noon, far back in the hills of central Texas, as my father and I sat together eating our sandwiches, he tried to console me.

"Don't be too hard on yourself, son," he said. "Everyone misses at first. Next time you get a shot, take a deep breath, aim carefully, and then squeeze the trigger." It was advice he had given me repeatedly through the years I had been learning to handle a rifle.

Later that afternoon, a seven-point buck jumped out ahead of my dad and plunged into a grove of scrub oak trees. "He's coming your way!" I heard my father call. Suddenly, about eighty yards in front of me, the buck burst out into a clearing. All I remember was the sound of my rifle and the buck falling.

"I got him, Dad!" I cried. "I got him!"

I was bending over the deer counting the points on his antlers when my father joined me. I will never forget the sound of his voice as he hugged me and said, "Son, I'm proud of you!" It was about the greatest day in my life. Not just because I had bagged my first buck, but because I had successfully applied the skill my father had imparted to me and he was proud of me.

Even as I type these words nearly a half-century later, the memory of my father's approbation warms my heart once more. If anyone were to ask me—then or now—what was most memorable about killing my first deer, I would have to say, "The knowledge that I had pleased my father."

One of the obvious truths about the life and ministry of our Lord Jesus was that He lived to please the Father. Jesus said, "For I always do what pleases him" (John 8:29).

In a very real sense, Jesus' ministry was an expression of the training He received from the Father through the Holy Spirit.

I tell you the truth, the Son can do nothing by himself; he can do only what he sees his Father doing, because whatever the Father does the Son also does. For the Father loves the Son and shows him all he does.

John 5:19–20

Not much makes a man happier than to have his son achieve some worthy goal or conduct himself in some exemplary way, simply because he desires to please and honor his father. Our heavenly Father was no different in regard to His own Son. On at least four occasions in the Gospels, we read that the Father spoke from heaven, declaring His approbation. In Matthew 3:17, for example, He says, "This is my Son, whom I love; with him I am well pleased."

Reduced to simplest terms, the primary responsibility of every believer is to live a life pleasing to the Father. Of course, we won't always succeed, but that should be our goal. I didn't always succeed in doing those things that pleased my earthly father, but I was a far happier son when my days were spent in ways designed to win his approval.

I'm not sure there is a more satisfying feeling in the whole world than the one that comes to a child when he knows he has succeeded in pleasing his father. And nothing makes the heart of a father happier—either our father on earth or our Father in heaven—than a child who has set his heart to do those things that please him.

18

Some People
Are Funny That Way

Sometimes it's amazing the length Christians will go to in their determination to defend their theologies (read that, prejudices!). I have been in the deliverance ministry—the ministry of casting out demons—for almost twenty years, and have seen literally thousands of tormented believers set free by the power of the Holy Spirit. It is a ministry authorized by Scripture, widely accepted in the charismatic renewal, and one that has found favor in churches of almost every denomination.

Yet there are millions of sincere Christians, theologians, ministers, Bible teachers, and laymen alike, who fiercely argue that deliverance is not for today. Besides, they say, "Christians can't have demons. Oh, demons can *harass* Christians, demons can *attack* Christians, they can even be *on* Christians, but demons cannot be *in* Christians."

At a recent leadership retreat, two outstanding men of God, both from religious traditions that reject deliverance for Christians, came to the retreat in great personal need. Both were being severely harassed by the devil and both asked for prayer. A young evangelist experienced in casting out demons was asked to pray for them. He prayed for the first man, rebuking Satan and commanding the evil spirits tormenting him to depart. Acknowledging the immediate relief he received, the man simply ignored his theology and humbly expressed his gratitude.

The second man then knelt before the evangelist for prayer. Again Satan was rebuked and the tormenting spirits were commanded to leave, and again the relief was evident. But as the grateful theologian rose from his knees, his theological prejudice reasserted itself.

"Remember," he said to the evangelist and to those of us sitting nearby, "those demons were *on,* not *in.*"

The young evangelist smiled and said, "All right, you demons, come out or come off—whichever!"

Later, I expressed my gratitude to the young man for the tact and humor he used in handling the situation. I laughed and said, "You may be entering a whole new phase of ministry—casting *off* demons in the name of Jesus!"

The problem some people have accepting the idea that Christians can need deliverance from evil spirits stems from the habit of referring to Spirit-*baptized* believers as Spirit-*filled* believers. If we were Spirit-*filled* all the time, there would never be any room for an evil spirit. But Spirit-baptized does not necessarily mean Spirit-filled. As one who has received the baptism in the Holy Spirit, I can truthfully say at any time, "I am a Spirit-baptized believer in Jesus Christ." But I cannot truthfully say that I am always a Spirit-*filled* believer. Any time I become angry or impatient or slothful or critical, I can lay no legitimate claim to being full of the Holy Spirit.

Someone has wisely suggested, "If you want to know if you're really filled with the Holy Spirit, check and see what spills over when you're jostled." If we are really *full* of the Holy Spirit, when someone says something mean and nasty to us, it will be the Holy Spirit who spills over. We will automatically respond with something like, "Praise God! I was just hoping the Lord would send me someone to pray for, and He has sent you. God bless you."

But if what jostles over is a furious, "Just who do you think you are, talking to me like that?" then we may be Spirit-baptized, but certainly we aren't Spirit-filled. At least not right then.

Acts 2:4 tells how the disciples were all "filled with the Holy Spirit and began to speak in other tongues." Later, in Acts 4:31, they were all "filled with the Holy Spirit and spoke the word of God boldly." If they were "filled" in Acts 2, why did they need to be "filled" again in Acts 4?

Someone once asked the great evangelist Dwight L. Moody why he testified to having been filled with the Holy Spirit so many times.

He responded, "The answer is simple: I leak!"

And so do we all.

19

The Best Use
of My Time

Our age is characterized by a preoccupation with saving time. Yet no matter how much time we save, no one seems to have enough. The truth is, time can't be saved; it can only be spent. And how we spend it makes all the difference.

In his book *Walden*, Henry David Thoreau wrote, "Time is but the stream I go a-fishing in." Significantly, his book—a classic in American literature—is a product of two years he "squandered" living at the edge of Walden Pond, frittering away his time meditating and daydreaming, recording thoughts and insights that have changed and enriched millions of lives for more than 150 years. Of course, he could have spent those years working hard at something the world considers useful, such as making money.

King David also spent much of his time in useless activity. The shepherd king was not only a mighty warrior but also a poet and daydreamer who wasted days and weeks obeying his God who said, "Be still, and know that I am God . . ." (Psalm 46:10). If he hadn't we wouldn't have the book of Psalms.

Must we be "busy" to spend time profitably? Most Christians

seem to think so. Some years ago, a major magazine conducted a survey of forty thousand church members, the results of which showed that the average church member expected his pastor to spend eighty-four hours a week at his job.

During my years as a denominational pastor, I often felt that kind of pressure. But I thank God He gave me the courage to keep my priorities straight and not sacrifice my wife and children on the altar of my "ministerial career."

Recently, while going through some old files, I found a copy of a December 1961 church newsletter, written while I was pastor in Toronto. My comments on the minister's page expressed the struggle I had in taking an hour of a busy day and spending it with my son.

> The other day I came home to find our four-year-old son, Glenn, fascinated by the snow. As I put on my coat to return to work after lunch, he put on his coat and boots to go outside and build a snowman. Now, grown-ups are too busy to build snowmen. Everyone knows that, even my son. So he didn't ask for my help, and maybe that's why I decided to help him build one.

> It was a terribly inefficient and undignified way for a minister to behave right in broad daylight. I could have spent the time more profitably doing something else. For most people, that's what time is for—to make a profit. But I'm not sure that my time with my son was time wasted. I believe I made a deposit in a different kind of bank, and the memory of my son's laughter and his shiny-eyed wonder as Jolly Jim the Snowman took shape, bears me out. The world's a better place, my son's a better boy, and I'm a better father because of Jolly Jim, even though he didn't live too long.

> In the late afternoon, I returned home to find that some schoolboy, whose parents had already convinced him that the world has no time or place for a snowman, had come along and knocked Jolly Jim's head off. He hadn't had time to build a snowman; he only had time to wreck one. But for

my son and me, the memory our time together in building
Jolly Jim remains intact. No one can tear that down.

Today I'm proud of the man my son has become, married and
with a son and daughter of his own.

Looking back, I know I had my priorities straight that December day. Some people driving past the parsonage may have
thought they saw a minister neglecting his church duties to frit-
ter away his time helping his four-year-old son build a snowman
at noon. But what they really saw was a man busily engaged in
one of the most noble tasks God ever assigned: they saw a father
taking time to build his son.

Do we need to save more time? No, we need more people to
spend their time in ways that will bear fruit in future generations.

— 20

Portrait of a Phony

Most seminary graduates enter their first full-time pastorate longing to lead their congregation to new and more noble heights. They are soon dismayed, however, to find people prone to applying their sermons to everyone but themselves, and the board of elders determined to resist fresh pastoral vision and insight at all costs.

Sadly, such resistance often indicates a prideful satisfaction that eventually leads to phoniness. My dictionary defines a phony as one whose life is "marked by empty pretension," a "fake."

A ministerial survey in the denomination I served revealed the average preacher left the ministry after seven years and two pastorates. I believe most men left because they were fed up with the phoniness, a phoniness all the more devastating to the Body of Christ because those who suffer from it so often seem so oblivious to their condition.

Through the years I've met my share of phonies. An elder in a church I pastored years ago could pray prayers that moved people to tears. But for more than twenty-five years he had dominated the whole congregation by his narrow convictions and violent temper. Once, when I confronted him about his anger, he flew into an even greater rage. "That's not anger," he roared.

"That's righteous indignation!" My challenge didn't help at all. He didn't change, and I ended up with a nervous stomach and high blood pressure. Phony! Hypocrite!

Then there was the woman so wealthy she could have bought the church seven times over and never missed the money, but she contributed only fifty dollars a year. On the first Sunday of every year she came to church to deposit her check in the offering plate "to set a good example for the others." Phony! Hypocrite!

I also remember a prosperous businessman who boasted he had no need to tithe, because "I'm a Christian and everything I have already belongs to God." Phony! Hypocrite!

Phoniness was a problem in Jesus' day as well. It's interesting to note that when priests were so numerous they had to cast lots to see who would serve in the Temple, Jesus didn't choose a single one as a disciple. Of course, Jesus didn't call the priests phonies, He called them hypocrites, which means the same thing.

According to the dictionary, a hypocrite is "one who affects virtues or qualities he does not have." In Matthew 23 Jesus called the religious leaders hypocrites seven times and then added a few additional phrases, such as "sons of hell," "blind guides," "whitewashed tombs full of dead men's bones," and "brood of vipers," just so there would be no mistaking His true opinion of them.

Jesus also exposed phonies in His parable about the Pharisee and the tax collector in Luke 18. The Pharisee boasted, "God, I thank you that I am not like all other men . . ." (verse 11), and his prayer went no higher than the top of his head. But the tax collector, who prayed humbly, "God, have mercy . . ." (verse 13), "returned home justified" when his simple prayer touched the heart of God.

The humble and the hypocrite; the pure in heart and the phonies! My own experience confirms that the Kingdom of God nourishes both, like wheat and tares growing side by side. It has been my privilege through the years to serve with hundreds of faithful men and women who love the Lord, and who daily acknowledge their dependence on His mercy. But I've also known—and sometimes ministered with—others who mouth the right words but who are so smug and self-righteous that it is an embarrassment to be around them.

On the surface phoniness seems harmless enough. But the hypocrite can be so jealous of his place and reputation that he will kill to preserve them, claiming all the while he's doing God a favor (see John 16:2). The scribes and Pharisees were so furious when Jesus exposed their phoniness that they plotted and carried out His murder.

God hates phonies. I believe He grieves over them because He can neither bless them nor use them, and because He knows sooner or later they will inflict great harm on the Body of Christ.

But thank God for all the humble little people who—without phoniness—service Him so faithfully. Jesus called them the salt of the earth. And that's the kind of people with which He's building His Kingdom.

21

Because He Says So

When I was growing up, I frequently complained about having to obey my parents. My favorite protest began, "I don't see why I have to . . ."

Dad's response to my complaint was always quick and consistent: "Because I say so, that's why!" And through the years I learned my dad's word could be trusted. Whether he was demanding obedience or making a promise, he meant what he said.

I preached a sermon not long ago in Mobile, Alabama, about learning to trust God, and the message seemed to encourage some people. Of course, I was preaching to myself as well as to the congregation, since as a Christian my greatest challenge continues to be how to trust God. I suspect the same thing is true of many of you.

Our major battle in spiritual warfare rages around that struggle. God encourages us to believe Him, the devil entices us to believe him, and we must choose between the two. As my old friend Rufus Moseley was fond of saying, "God is always voting for us; the devil is always voting against us; and the way we vote carries the election."

The truth is, man's problems on earth began when he started

to doubt God's word. Adam and Eve had it made until the serpent tricked Eve into doubting God's word. "Did God really say . . ."

Trusting God.

How can something that sounds so simple be so hard?

One of my favorite Bible stories is the one where Peter walks on the water. There he is, striding over the waves, heading straight for Jesus, when suddenly doubts assail and he begins to sink. When he cries for help, Jesus grabs him by the hand and hauls him back on top of the waves, saying, "You of little faith, why did you doubt?" (Matthew 14:31).

We can forgive Peter for not pausing at that particular moment to give Jesus a carefully thought-out reply. But back in the boat he might have pondered the question, "Why did I doubt?" He may have even remembered another day when his faith was put to the test, the day he was first called to be a disciple. That was the day Jesus came and sat in his boat to preach to the people. Then afterward, He said to Peter, "Put out into deep water, and let down the nets for a catch" (Luke 5:4).

Sometime before this Peter had rejoiced when Jesus healed his mother-in-law, and I'm sure he had rejoiced to see Jesus cast out demons and heal the sick. But now, with his own faith being put to the test by Jesus' command to move to deeper water and let down the nets, it wasn't so easy to believe.

After all, Jesus knew all about God and man, but Peter knew all about fish and fishing. And right then, fishing wasn't all that good! He told Jesus so.

"Master, we've worked hard all night and haven't caught anything . . ." (Luke 5:5).

The Bible doesn't say, but I believe Peter's first response was followed by a long pause. I think Jesus just sat there in the boat, looking at Peter and waiting—along with James and John and the crowd on the shore. All of them waiting to see what the big fisherman would do.

Well, Peter said and did exactly the right thing: he acted on the word of God.

"... But because you say so, I will let down the nets" (verse 5).

You know what happened. The nets encircled so many fish that two boats couldn't hold the catch. Peter fell on his knees and asked Jesus to forgive him for doubting.

Peter wasn't always that faithful or that fortunate. All his life he struggled to believe, just as we do. But the Lord was patient with Peter, just as He is with us. Even when we're tired of hauling in empty nets, He wants us to know His word can still be trusted. Because He says so, let's push out into deeper waters this time and try again. He still knows where the fish are.

22

From Tragedy
to Triumph

By any reasonable standards, Jim and Barbara Hoffer's situation was not just desperate; it was hopeless. As we drove to their home, their pastor, Kelly Cahill, explained.

Shorty before their marriage three years before, Jim received the devastating news that he had Lou Gehrig's disease, an incurable illness that systematically destroys the nervous system, leading to progressive paralysis and death. Jim and Barbara decided to marry anyway, but the disease followed its relentless course and within two years Jim was confined to a wheelchair, unable to move or speak.

Providentially, the Hoffers met Kelly and through his care and ministry they became Christians. Nevertheless, Jim's physical condition continued to deteriorate. He and Barbara had read some of my books, and when they learned from their pastor that I was to be in the area, they asked if I could visit them.

It was a cold, dreary day with a mixture of rain and sleet falling as we arrived at their home in Diamondale, Michigan. I prepared myself for the depressing atmosphere one usually finds surrounding those who are terminally ill. But to my surprise the home was bright and cheery with plants and pleasant decorations tastefully arranged amid the special medical equipment and furniture required for Jim's care. Moreover, an amazing peace seemed to permeate their home.

Barbara called a greeting to us from the next room. After a few minutes she wheeled her husband in, and I stood to one side as she and Kelly lifted Jim from his wheelchair and strapped him upright in a special seat. The sight of his thin, wasted form almost swallowed by his pajamas and his hands folded helplessly in his lap aroused deep sympathy in me. After brushing his hair and adjusting the feeding tube in his nose, Barbara turned to me with a smile.

"Reverend Basham, I want you to meet my husband, Jim." From the quiet pride in her voice, Jim could have been president of General Motors. I said hello, and when Jim's eyes met mine, I knew why there was such peace in that home.

Jim Hoffer's eyes were filled with the light of heaven.

For the next half hour we talked about life and death and heaven and earth as easily as most people chat about the weather. Somehow, the peace surrounding Jim and Barbara made such conversation seem particularly right and appropriate. Of course, Kelly, Barbara, and I did most of the talking, because Jim's only means of communication consisted of staring at printed letters carefully arranged on a large, clear plastic shield that Kelly or Barbara would hold in front of him. Gazing at the letters one at a time, he slowly spelled out the words.

"Thank-you-for-coming," he said. And a little later, "God-is-so-good-to-me." His longest sentence was the most amazing of all.

"My-illness-has-brought-many-blessings." When Kelly repeated his words aloud for confirmation, Jim's eyes shone with added joy.

In more than thirty-five years of ministry, I have never shared in circumstances so helpless yet so triumphant. Barbara had even been forced to quit her job to provide total care for Jim, leaving them with practically no income. Yet her own serenity and confidence fully matched her husband's.

As I watched Jim struggle to communicate, his radiant spirit seemed almost impatient to leave the tired and wasted body in which it was contained. It was as if he had already entered the resurrection life that Paul speaks about in 1 Corinthians 15: "Death has been swallowed up in victory. . . . Where, O death, is your sting?" (verses 54–55).

Before we left we prayed together, but it seemed almost unnecessary; God was already present with such love and power. As we walked to the car, I said, "Kelly, I thought I was coming here to minister, but I was mistaken. God brought me here to be ministered to."

Meeting Jim and Barbara simply strengthened my conviction that our destiny is the Kingdom of God—whether on earth or in heaven is simply a matter of geography. Through his illness, Jim Hoffer found the Kingdom here on earth. And several months after we met he moved on to the one in heaven. For him, it was such a small step.

23

Sometimes,
Just to Endure Is Victory

Occasionally, even during the toughest of times, you may hear a word from God that makes all the difference—just the word you need to see you through. Not long ago just such a word came to me.

It had been a long week filled with nothing but frustrations and hassles. Too weary to pray and too bruised to be spiritual, Alice and I sat together on the couch, numbly grateful for having slipped sideways through the day with no new crisis erupting.

"Whatever happened to the victorious Christian life?" I sighed aloud.

Alice reached over and squeezed my hand. "Honey," she said, *"sometimes, just to endure is victory."*

It was a truth so simple yet so encouraging I knew it had to be from God.

Too often we act as if being a faithful Christian requires a string of answered prayers or an unbroken series of spiritual successes. But God has called us to be faithful, not successful. Although it is true that most Christian testimonies affirm God's power to bring us from sin to salvation, from sickness to health, or from poverty to prosperity, we need to keep in mind that instantaneous transformations by His grace are more the exception than the rule.

My old friend Rufus Moseley used to say, "God is a bit sparing with His miracles. If there weren't any, we'd all be goners, but if there were too many, we'd all become lazy."

Miracles may take us to the mountaintop, but endurance is needed in the valleys. In fact, there can be no mountain peaks without valleys in between. Testimony to miracles notwithstanding, the Bible abounds with verses calling for endurance.

After warning of the perils and hardships of "the last days," Jesus concludes, "But the one who *endures* to the end, he shall be saved" (Matthew 24:13, NAS). In 1 Corinthians 13:7 (NAS), Paul says that love "*endures* all things," and in 2 Timothy 4:5 (NAS) that we must "*endure* hardship." James says, "We count those blessed who *endured*" (James 5:11, NAS, italics added).

So while there are those spectacular victories that reflect the miraculous intervention of God, far more often it is by faithful endurance that we obtain eventual victory.

Let me discourage no one from praying for miracles. The Scriptures urge us to believe God for them, and I pray for them all the time. I know the joy that comes with seeing the power of the Holy Spirit move in a miraculous way. But let not our desire for miracles blind us to the availability of quiet daily grace, which—like manna to the Israelites—can strengthen us for enduring trials we cannot escape and wrestling with difficulties we cannot cast aside.

Perhaps even now, you may be at a place where you feel hemmed in by walls too high to leap over, or surrounded by mountains of difficulty that your faith can't seem to move—with no sign of a miracle anywhere on the horizon. I know the feeling well. But finding yourself in such a narrow place is no reason to grieve, nor does being there signify failure or defeat. God is still present with grace to endure. After all, some walls are meant for leaning on rather than leaping over, and some mountains are meant for climbing rather than "casting." Some of life's experiences are destined to be endured rather than enjoyed.

So during those long and unyielding days when quick answers and happy solutions are nowhere to be found, why not lean into the Lord and accept His comforting reminder: "Sometimes, just to endure is victory." It may prove just the right word to see you through.

— 24

Spend
Your Words Wisely

"... For out of the overflow of the heart the mouth
speaks."   Matthew 12:34

Genesis 1 tells us how God created the heavens and the earth:
God *said* it, and it happened! He *spoke* all creation into existence.
God's Word is an extension of His own creative nature. Genesis
also tells us that God made man in His own image and likeness.
Therefore our words, too, are extensions of ourselves, having
within them the potential to build up or tear down, to create or
destroy. No wonder Jesus said that on the Day of Judgment men
will have to give an account for all they have said (see Matthew
12:36–37).

It is a sobering exercise to consider what words can do, to
contemplate the power of the tongue. The little book of James
devotes an entire chapter to our inability to tame the tongue. "If
anyone is never at fault in what he says, he is a perfect man, able

to keep his whole body in check" (James 3:2). In other words, mastery of the tongue signifies mastery of the whole person.

James goes on to say:

Consider what a great forest is set on fire by a small spark. The tongue also is a fire, a world of evil among the parts of the body. It corrupts the whole person, sets the whole course of his life on fire, and is itself set on fire by hell.

James 3:5–6

James makes it plain that evil speaking not only injures those it is directed against, but it can literally destroy the person who uses it. When we indulge in critical, accusing talk, we seldom consider the devastating spiritual effect it is having on us. Evil talk is like a boomerang. We speak it only to have it return to inflict its greatest injury on ourselves. Paul stated it just as clearly another way: "Do not be deceived: God cannot be mocked. *A man reaps what he sows* (Galatians 6:7, italics added).

Unfortunately, most of us are only dimly aware of the power of our words. We have a terrible freedom to use our words to create a hell or a heaven. We can speak hateful, fearful, doubtful words—words that enrage, torment, and destroy. We can speak words of envy and spite, wicked words that slander and betray, and in the process minister death to ourselves and those to whom we speak.

Or we can speak truthful, grateful, joyful words—words that comfort, heal, encourage, and strengthen. We can speak words of faith, hope, and love; blessed covenantal words that forgive, redeem, and restore, and in the process minister life to ourselves and those to whom we speak.

If words were dollars, we would all be millionaires because we have access to an unlimited supply of them to gather and spend however we choose. But we gather from two different storehouses, and we spend two kinds of currency. We can draw our words from one source, using them to darken the day as mouth-pieces for the devil, spreading his garbage of suspicion and hatred all over creation and soiling our own souls in the process. Or we can draw our words from the other Source, using them to light up the day as philanthropists of hope, lavishing praise, encouragement, and faith with royal extravagance on every person we meet, enriching his or her life and our own souls in the process.

One way we serve the prince of darkness and the evil kingdoms of this world; the other way we serve the Prince of Peace and the Kingdom of God on earth.

25

Just As I Am

Back when I was a seminary student and preaching on weekends in a little Kansas church, a deaconess came up to me after the service one Sunday and said, "I really want to be a Christian, but I'm never sure I'm doing enough to get into heaven."

I was blunt and rather tactless, but I had the right answer. "No, Clara," I replied. "You are not doing enough to get to heaven, and you never will!"

Then I had to explain to the surprised woman how salvation comes by faith, not by works, and that we get to heaven by trusting, not by trying.

I'm not sure I convinced her.

Like millions of other sincere people who "believe in God and try to do right," Clara was putting her faith in the wrong person. She wanted to prove to God she was worthy and, therefore, earn her own way to heaven.

For people like Clara, the Gospel is too good to be true. They say, "Yes, I know Jesus died on the Cross for my sins, *but* . . ." and then proceed to list any number of additional things they must do—just in case what He did was not enough.

But salvation is a gift we receive by faith, not a reward we earn by trying to be good. Our good works are a response *to* our salvation, not a requirement *for* it. Martin Luther once said, "To claim your salvation by works is to kick Jesus Christ in the teeth!"

In Luke 18:9–14, Jesus told "some who were confident of their own righteousness" a parable about two men: a Pharisee who thanked God that he was not like other men and a tax collector who simply cried for mercy. The Pharisee believed the good he had done made him righteous, while the tax collector simply confessed he was a sinner and pled for mercy. Yet it was not the Pharisee but the tax collector whom Jesus honored.

I've been a Christian for over half a century now, and I've discovered that the trouble most people have trying to be Christian is that they try to be Christian by trying. But being Christian doesn't come by trying, it comes by trusting. This is the heart of the Gospel. Miss this and you miss it all.

> For it is by grace you have been saved, through faith—*and this not from yourselves,* it is the gift of God—*not by works,* so that no one can boast.
>
> Ephesians 2:8–9, italics added

Looking back, I would have to say the most difficult times in my own life have been those brief, foolish periods when I have tried to trust in my own righteousness. But reputation, achievement, good behavior, ministry, service—none of them ever earned me one ounce of justification. I'm still a sinner saved by grace.

I remember a spring Sunday morning in 1934, when as a boy of eight, I walked down the aisle of the First Baptist Church in Wichita Falls and surrendered my life to Jesus Christ. I remember how sinful I felt, and how grateful that Jesus loved me anyway. And when I timidly confessed my faith in Him before that large congregation, I knew something wonderful had happened—I knew that He had forgiven me and accepted me.

I also remember the words of the hymn that the congregation

was singing as I went forward. They are still the only acceptable basis for my salvation—or for yours.

> *Just as I am, without one plea,*
> *But that Thy blood was shed for me,*
> *And that Thou bidd'st me come to Thee,*
> *O Lamb of God I come! I come!*

That's the way the Lord first showed it to me over fifty years ago, and that's still the way I see it.

26

Preach on Love, Or I'll Hit You with My Bible!

There's a quirk in human nature we all suffer from. It's our amazing ability to be certain that what we believe is right, just because we believe it. This is especially true of our religious convictions. We are so sure they are correct, we want them all set in concrete, never to be tampered with, never to change. And it seems the more Bible-believing we are, the more certain we are about our convictions.

We even take pride in becoming offended when someone with a different truth or revelation challenges those convictions. That's one reason why Bible teachers like me periodically face overheated critics who have become disturbed about something we said or wrote.

In a Bible conference in Ohio a few years ago, I was teaching several lessons on the gifts of the Holy Spirit. The audience was about equally divided between charismatic Christians and non-charismatic Christians, between those who believed the supernatural gifts of the Holy Spirit were available to believers today and those who did not.

At the close of my message on the gift of tongues, I saw an attractive, but agitated young woman bearing down on me, open Bible in hand. Since I could almost see the steam coming out of her ears, I knew I was in for a verbal shellacking.

Smiling sweetly at her, I said, "Do you have a question about something I said in my teaching?"

She shoved her open Bible right up under my nose and began jabbing the page with an offended index finger. I wasn't surprised to see she was gouging 1 Corinthians 13.

"I want to know why you didn't read this chapter," her voice was full of accusation. "You read chapters 12 and 14, but you deliberately ignored chapter 13!"

"You are absolutely right," I agreed. "That's because in chapter 13 Paul is teaching about love. But don't you remember? I didn't teach on love tonight, I taught on the gift of speaking in tongues. And Paul doesn't talk about that gift in chapter 13; he deals with it in chapters 12 and 14."

But what seemed to be a logical explanation to me, infuriated her all the more.

"Paul said love is the most important thing!" Her voice rose about half an octave. "The church needs more love! Why don't you teach on love? All that talk about speaking in tongues just gets everyone upset! Jesus said we're to show love to one another!"

I couldn't resist a response I knew would only make matters worse.

"You mean like the love you are showing me right now?"

That really tore it! She glared at me as she slammed her Bible shut. For a moment I thought she was going to swat me on the side of my head with it. Instead, she whirled around and stalked up the auditorium aisle, angry high heels denting the floor with every step.

As I watched her go, I thought once again how difficult it is for Christians to disagree agreeably. I recalled the many times during the years that people have become upset over something I have taught or written. Thankfully, some critics whose lives and convictions changed later on came and apologized and asked forgiveness. "You aren't as crazy as we first thought," they said. I'm sure they thought that would make me feel better.

The older I get the more I want to be tolerant and forgiving. But since I'm human, I still resent it when people imply that I'm either a heretic or a false prophet. I know Scripture says, "Love your enemies and pray for those who persecute you" (Matthew 5:44). And I believe we should all try to do that—if we can.

But Scripture also says, "Vengeance is mine; I will repay, saith the Lord" (Romans 12:19, KJV). And it also says that on earth, God uses delegated human authority (see Romans 13).

So in my weaker moments, I confess I have a secret dream—a dream that one day a group of believers who feel called to exercise God's delegated authority will form a Christian "hit squad," and will then proceed to wreak vengeance for the Lord by permanently eradicating certain of His critics—and mine!

Only, then I recall how I have preached some sermons and taught some Bible lessons through the years that deserved to be criticized. Immature, needlessly controversial messages that made me feel smug while I was "letting them have it!" but afterward left me wishing fervently that everyone who heard me would forgive me for what I said and forget I ever said it.

That's the trouble when you begin to criticize your critics. You know they may be wrong about some specific matters—just as you are. But deep down you also know that most of the time they are right about what they believe and don't believe—just as you are.

All of which means we need to have much more patience with one another, we need to have much more love for one another, and we need to be much more tolerant and much less critical of one another.

And you'd better completely agree with everything I have just said, or I'll hit you with my Bible!

— 27

Nobody Likes Me!

He hath made us accepted in the beloved.

Ephesians 1:6, KJV

Maturity is a highly desirable goal for every Christian. Yet there resides within each of us a kind of childlike trust and innocence that stubbornly resists growing up. Basically, that is a good thing. Jesus Himself said, "Unless you ... become like little children, you will never enter the kingdom of heaven" (Matthew 18:3).

When counseling young people who are about to get married, I often suggest that if they can only remember that inside every man lives a little boy and inside every woman lives a little girl, it will help them through some difficult times.

But being childlike also leaves us vulnerable to rejection. When we are criticized, misunderstood, or mistreated, we can't help feeling rejected. Even though we may try desperately to conceal our feelings, people can usually tell anyway. I remember a sarcastic little ditty the neighborhood kids used to sing when someone in our crowd was feeling sorry for himself:

Nobody likes me, everybody hates me,
I'm going out to eat worms!

It's bad enough when children are critical of their peers; it's far worse when parents voice cruel criticisms of their offspring. Many critical parents seem to have little conception of how important it is to love and encourage their children. I have even heard Christian parents boast about withholding love and approval from their children so they would "grow up tough and be able to live in the real world." But denying love and approval does not produce tough adults. Rather it produces emotional cripples who may suffer from rejection and low self-esteem their whole lives.

Even children who grow up in a loving and secure home can sometimes suffer feelings of rejection. I recall the time when our three-year-old daugher, Lisa, misbehaved in a way that called for a spanking. Afterward, she ran to her room, sobbing. But she knew where Ultimate Comfort lay. A few minutes later her mother and I heard a quavery little voice lift itelf in song:

"I am so glad that Jesus loves me,
Jesus loves me, Jesus loves me.
I am so glad that Jesus loves me,
Jesus loves even me."

Hearts melting, we rushed into her room and lifted her in our arms, saying, "We love you too, honey! We love you too!" And then we sang the chorus again, together.

When I teach on "The Importance of Approval and Praise," I often tell audiences that our human anatomy contains a secret part that I call a "praise receptacle" or an "approval bucket." All of us have one; it's located somewhere near the heart. And we are constantly seeking the love, the acceptance, and the approval of friends and family to fill it up. When that approval bucket is full, we bloom and prosper. When it is empty, we wither and die inside. Even Jesus needed to hear His Father say, "This is my Son, whom I love; with him I am well pleased" (Matthew 3:17).

But since so many situations seemed designed to overturn our approval bucket, it's difficult to keep it full! I will never forget the emotional struggle I went through trying to get my first book published.

I sent the manuscript to publisher after publisher only to receive it back with the standard rejection slip that stated, "We are sorry, but this material does not meet our publishing needs at this time." The standard printed rejection was bad enough, but one editor's negative response almost did me in. Not content with the standard rejection slip, he sent me a hostile personal letter telling me why he did not like my book and why he did not think it deserved to be published. His letter ended with a sarcastic suggestion: "Why don't you reduce this manuscript to a magazine article and submit it to some publication whose readers believe this kind of stuff you are writing about?"

After three years of writing and editing a 200-page manuscript in which I bared my soul, only to be told to reduce it to a magazine article—you can imagine the humiliation and rejection I felt! I slogged around in an emotional pit for two weeks. It didn't help that I had recently read an article about a despondent author who shot himself. Beside the body, the police found a manuscript with a rejection slip attached that read, "This manuscript stinks!"

When my book did find a publisher some months later, I had to resist the strong temptation to send a copy to that editor, with a letter equally nasty as his, telling him how wrong I thought he had been!

There are not many things man longs for more than acceptance and approval. From childhood to old age, we shrink from rejection. Yet, since rejection is an inevitable part of life, learning to face it positively helps build character. It is also important to remember that since Jesus died to reconcile us to God, even when we seem to find rejection everywhere else, we are still acceptable to Him.

Once a group of us prayed for a widow who was suffering great heartache and loneliness. As we prayed, the love of God suddenly flooded her being. Her face lit up with joy as her arms went up over her head, and she began to sing spontaneous praises to God.

When the time of worship ended, she fell back in her chair with tears of happiness streaming down her cheeks. Then she looked up at us and exclaimed, "Oh, I feel so *accepted!*"

Once we accept by faith the glorious truth that "He hath made us accepted in the beloved," it's much easier to cope with those days when it seems no one cares about us but Him.

28

The Perils of a Purple Plymouth

Do not think of yourself more highly than you ought, but rather think of yourself with sober judgment, in accordance with the measure of faith God has given you.

Romans 12:3

It was February 1957. I had just begun my first full-time pastorate in a small church in Washington, D.C., and was shopping for a new car. During seminary years in Oklahoma, a plain green Studebaker had faithfully carried me and my family more than 137,000 miles between Bible college and weekend ministry at my student church. But I was convinced that any young minister bent on becoming a great spiritual leader in the nation's capital needed more appropriate transportation. While we really did need a new car, it was the overinflated appraisal of my new status that prompted my folly.

You may be too young to remember that 1957 was the year of the tail fin in U.S. car design. I chose a slick burgundy (read that, purple!) Plymouth with ivory stripes down its sides and tail fins that soared above the rear bumper. Even parked at the curb it looked as if it were traveling 80 m.p.h. What's more, it had plush carpeting and *push-button* automatic transmission.

With my mind already made up, I prayed fervently to know the will of God. I claimed a dozen different scriptural promises and rebuked all the devil's negative thoughts—thoughts of how the payments would strain our frail budget and how the car I had in mind seemed more appropriate for a college playboy than a conservative pastor.

The day I signed the sales contract—a day I later called "the beginning of sorrows"—I ripped a three-inch tear in my best slacks on a sharp corner of the salesman's desk. I suspected God might be trying to get my attention, but I bought the car anyway.

I drove my new purple Plymouth out into rush-hour traffic and stalled right in front of the dealership. They had neglected to put gasoline in the car.

I marched back inside to complain.

I didn't discover the ripped seams in the rear seat upholstery until I got home and was showing the new car to my wife.

I drove the car back to the dealer to complain.

The next morning I found a large puddle of transmission fluid on the driveway, and my new car would not shift out of low gear.

I drove the car—all the way in low gear—back to the dealer to complain.

On the fifth day, I found a line of distortion running the entire width of the front windshield.

I drove the car back to the dealer to complain.

They replaced the windshield, then the car leaked when it rained.

I drove the car back to the dealer to complain.

The following week the front seat stopped adjusting properly, locking only all the way forward or all the way back, so I had to drive either with the steering wheel bumping my abdomen, or grasping the wheel at arm's length.

I drove the car back to the dealer to complain.

I also said if they still had my 1953 green Studebaker on the lot, I'd like to trade it back. They thought I was joking. I wasn't.

After the third trip to the service department with the new car, I found myself talking only to mechanics who mostly mumbled and looked at the floor. The service manager never seemed to be available. But I wasn't fooled. Deep down I knew that every time he saw that purple Plymouth and its wild-eyed driver approaching, the coward locked himself in the washroom.

If I said that things finally got better, I'd be lying. They never did. After fifteen exasperating months, I traded my 1957 purple lemon for a plain vanilla variety, with no carpet, no push-button transmission, and no tail fins; just dependable transportation appropriate for a young preacher in his first pastorate.

Is there a moral in all this? Yes, there is. God will allow us to have our own foolish way simply because it's often the most effective way of teaching us that His ways are better.

Rock Throwing
vs. Breeze Blowing

He stirs up his breezes, and the waters flow.

Psalm 147:18

"The wind blows wherever it pleases. You hear its sound, but you cannot tell where it comes from or where it is going."

John 3:8

It was a scorching summer afternoon twenty-five years ago. On vacation from my pastorate in Toronto, I was standing beside a pond of water located on my father-in-law's farm in Texas. Not a breath of wind was stirring and the pond's mirrored surface reflected an exact image of the searing sky above. Reverting to a childhood sport, I picked up a small stone from the shore, threw it toward the center of the pond and watched the smooth surface of the water break into a sudden pattern of concentric, ever-widening circles.

Then on impulse, I gathered a whole handful of stones and

began to hurl them one after another into the pond until its entire surface was covered with a changing pattern of overlapping, ever-widening rings. But I soon discovered that the only way I could keep the surface of the water alive was by continuing to throw stones. When my arm grew weary and my stone supply dwindled away, I stopped throwing to watch the last circling ripples recede into the shoreline and the pond reassume its placid surface.

Just like all the years of my ministry, I thought. Trying to stir the complacency of the church by tossing into its calm waters every stone of prayer, faith, exhortation, teaching, and testimony about the reality of the Kingdom of God I could gather. At best, my efforts seemed to make only a few temporary ripples.

Yet I had not only read of times and places where God moved in mighty power, I had personally experienced the supernatural presence of God. Understandably, I longed for such a sovereign visitation in my own church.

But in my gloomy imagination that day—and with the charismatic renewal still in its infancy—the state of the whole Church of Jesus Christ seemed represented by the glassy surface of that prairie pond. I felt that until the wind of the Spirit moved, the Church would remain lifeless, its mirrored surface reflecting only whatever fleeting fads and influences drifted overhead.

Then, as I stood beside that placid pond, from somewhere a sudden breeze swept across the face of the water. In an instant its smooth surface disappeared beneath a thousand laughing, sunlit ripples that danced their way from one shore to the other. Lifeless only moments before, now the little pond sparkled with vitality and light. I felt God in that breeze. It was as if He were telling me that if He could do it with a pond, He could do it with people.

I returned to my church in Toronto encouraged, and the following spring a sudden breeze from the Holy Spirit swept into our midweek prayer meeting, bringing healing, deliverance, prophecies, dreams and visions, and transforming life to the handful of faithful believers who had prayed so patiently for its arrival.

In my years of ministry since, I've continued to throw my share of stones into lifeless ponds, and I suspect I've more to throw yet. But thank God, I've also been present many times and many places when the breeze of the Holy Spirit came to do its life-changing work.

So if in your current place in the Body of Christ, the water seems painfully still, with its only ripples the ones those made by you and a few other faithful saints, don't despair! God is faithful. Keep on tossing those stones, for somewhere not far away, fresh breezes are stirring and one of them may be heading your way.

30

That's Where
Martha Missed It

Some years ago I felt strongly urged by the Lord to give $150 to a fellow minister in need. I obeyed, even though at the time that $150 represented about 75 percent of my total financial resources. That simple act of doing what the Lord wanted was followed by months of unexpected prosperity.

A few years later, in a time of relative abundance, I gave $1,000 to another ministry I felt was worthy of support. But this time there was no flood of blessing in return. At first I felt resentful that God hadn't been impressed by my generosity. But eventually, I acknowledged that the second gift had been my idea, not God's. God *let* me give the gift, but He hadn't *told* me to give it.

One of the most important truths we must learn as Christians is that there is often a vast difference between what God *lets* us do and what He *wants* us to do. That truth is graphically illustrated in the story of Jesus' visit to the home of Mary and Martha, found in Luke 10:38–42.

When Jesus arrived at their home, the sisters' reactions were as different as night and day. Although the biblical account is terse, the picture of what happened is clear. Gentle Mary, wide-eyed with wonder, sat adoringly at Jesus' feet, drinking in every word He shared. But Martha, bent on preparing dinner, scurried from cupboard to stove to table, casting angry glances at her sister. Finally her resentment exploded.

"Lord, don't you care that my sister has left me to do the work by myself? Tell her to help me!" (verse 40).

In her indignation, Martha didn't realize what she was saying. She actually rebuked the Lord for not having his priorities straight! Didn't He know that commitment must be shown by hard work and not idle conversation? Couldn't He see that what she was doing was more important than what Mary was doing, that her serving took precedence over His sharing and Mary's listening?

"Lord, tell Mary to get up and go to work! She should be rushing around like me, all frantic and fuming to get things done. Instead, she just sits there quietly listening to You. It's time You set her straight about what's important!"

Mary and Martha viewed the visit of Jesus in totally different ways. Mary saw an opportunity to listen and learn from the Lord, while Martha saw an opportunity to prove what a devoted worker she was. Mary sought revelation; Martha sought commendation. Mary chose the grace of intimate fellowship; Martha chose to prove she was a good cook.

We must understand that Martha was not sinful, just shortsighted. It's not that good deeds and hard work don't count; it's only that they can never substitute for an open heart and a listening ear. Notice that even after gently correcting Martha, Jesus still didn't insist that she come and join them; He simply observed that what she was doing was second-best.

"Mary has chosen what is better," He said (verse 42).

Martha had a choice. She could continue doing what the Lord *let* her do, that is, rush around madly proving what a good hostess she was, or she could start doing what He *wanted* her to do—sit with her sister, Mary, and listen to what He had to say.

Poor Martha! She chose hard work over fellowship with the Lord. Why would anyone do that?

But to be honest, all of us periodically contend with that powerful "Martha syndrome." Sometimes the busier we become serving the Lord, the harder it becomes to appreciate Mary's perspective.

Perspective is the key to the whole matter. The Lord had one perspective (which Mary happily embraced) while Martha had another. Her determination to serve the Lord was an expression of *her* perspective, not the Lord's. *And that's where Martha missed it!*

Remember, there is often a vast difference between what God *lets* us do and what He *wants* us to do.

P.S. The essay above appeared in *New Wine* magazine in March 1985. There were a number of letters in response to the article, not all of them agreeing with my evaluation of Martha's problem. They made me realize just how strongly the Martha syndrome does affect us. Here is a portion of one letter from a lady whose name just happened to be Martha.

Dear Mr. Basham,

I enjoyed your column, "Martha Missed It," in the March issue. May I, however, speak a word in Martha's defense? Jesus and His disciples stopped at Martha's home after they had been walking some distance. They were probably tired, hungry, thirsty, and dirty. Even if the Lord only had the twelve with him, a crowd of thirteen showing up on your front doorstep unexpectedly is still a handful!

The Lord may very well have been willing to wait for dinner. But I'll bet the tired, hungry disciples weren't so easygoing. Scripture doesn't depict the twelve as exactly patient, understanding types. How many of them were leaning on Martha to hurry with food and drinks, and making little comments as she rushed around while Mary sat at the Lord's feet?

I'd like to pass on a little story, found by Thomas Merton in some ancient manuscripts and reprinted by him in *The Wisdom of the Desert*.

A certain brother came to Abbot Silvany at Mt. Sinai and seeing the hermits at work he exclaimed: "Why do you work for the bread that perisheth? Mary has chosen the better part, namely to sit at the feet of the Lord without working."

Then the Abbot said to one of the hermits, "Give the brother a book and let him read; put him in an empty cell."

At the ninth hour the brother who was reading began to look out to see if the Abbot was not going to call him to dinner.

Sometime later he went to the Abbot and said, "Did the brethren not eat today, Father?"

"Oh, yes, certainly," said the Abbot. "They just had dinner."

"Well, why did you not call me?" said the brother.

"You are a spiritual man," said the Abbot. "You don't need this food that perisheth. We have to work, but you have chosen the best part. You read all day long and can get along without food."

Hearing this, the brother said, "Forgive me, Father." And the Abbot said, "Martha is necessary to Mary. It was because Martha worked that Mary was able to be praised."

I think Martha deserves a better press!

Sincerely,
Martha

I appreciated Martha's letter and the pertinent story from Thomas Merton's book. They almost make me feel better about my own Martha syndrome. It's not that I don't sympathize with Martha in the Scriptures, or Martha who wrote the letter, or the Abbot in the story.

My problem is in trying to represent their position before the Lord. After all, *He's* the one who criticized Martha and commended Mary. So if Martha and Martha and the Abbot are right, and Jesus is wrong, then *He's* the One who needs to be corrected. But I'm just not quite sure how to go about doing that.

– 31

Supersaints Aren't So Bad, After All

As Jesus was saying these things, a woman in the crowd called out, "Blessed is the mother who gave you birth and nursed you." He replied, "Blessed rather are those who hear the word of God and obey it."

Luke 11:27–28

Did you ever notice that God puts up with some really strange characters? Like "supersaints," those extra-earnest Christians who genuinely love God, but who believe that a faithful Christian life should resemble boot camp. Determined to be at least 150% Christian, supersaints feel a divine calling to force-feed friends and neighbors a steady diet of scriptural pronouncements, religious advice, and personal testimony—totally unaware that their unctuous behavior in public makes other Christians want to swear in private. The lady in the Scripture we just quoted sounds like a supersaint. Determined to impress her friends and neighbors and Jesus, she interrupted Him right in the middle of a powerful teaching.

Jesus didn't criticize her, though. Instead, He used her pious posturing to make a point. I dearly wish I could behave that way when I'm around supersaints, I really do. But most of the time, they just drive me up the wall!

Well, at least, they used to.

Have you ever met a supersaint? Thankfully, their number is not too large. But in a traveling ministry like mine, the sheer numbers of believers you come in contact with make it statistically impossible to avoid them all.

I remember a supersaint couple who provided hospitality for me during a three-day seminar in a western state. From the moment at the airport when I climbed into their ten-year-old Volkswagen with its "Honk If You Love Jesus" bumper sticker, I knew I had fallen into the hands of *serious* believers!

Tired from a long plane ride, and facing a two-hour drive to their home, I hinted that I would like to catch a nap. But it was too late. They had already begun to tell me how God was using them—*Praise the Lord!*—to spread His Word in their city— *Hallelujah.* And how on the way to the airport, they had witnessed—*Thank You, Jeeesus*—to a poor sinner pumping gas at the station—*Glory be to God!*—where they stopped to fill up "the Lord's Chariot." (A ten-year-old Volkswagen?)

And had I praised God for the glorious weather? The forecast had called for rain, but—*Bless God!*—they rebuked the devil and now would you just look at that miraculous sunshine!

The bombardment of choruses, Scripture, exhortation, and testimony continued all the way home, right on into the guest bedroom with its open Bible on the night table, plus cassette player loaded with a Jimmy Swaggart tape.

For the next three days, I was deluged with a flood of pious platitudes, tedious testimony, and pompous prayers before meals (I could have sworn their cat bowed its head every time grace was said, but it may have been my imagination). Each night when we returned home from the meeting, there were pointed suggestions as to how my teaching—not that it wasn't quite good—*Praise the Lord!*—could be made more effective.

In the faint hope that my hosts might have been trying hard to be spiritual just for my sake, I attempted several times to steer the conversation around to unreligious subjects, but it didn't help. When I mentioned I liked to fish, the husband said he had enjoyed fishing too, until—*Bless God!*—he became a "fisher of men." And when I tried to talk about my children and grand-children and his wife gazed at the ceiling and responded with her "*Hallelujah*—we're *all* children of our heavenly Father!" I found myself wistfully longing for the company of quiet sinners.

The three-day seminar finally ended and my stay at the super-saintly home mercifully drew to a close. As we arrived back at the airport, I was preparing to mention—redemptively, if possi-ble—the problem of their super-spirituality, when something happened that undid me altogether.

Before I could begin, I noticed my host was quiet for the first time in three days. With sudden tears in his eyes, he began tell-ing me how for years he and his wife had been frustrated church people with little real faith. Then someone gave them a copy of one of my books and they were both so blessed while reading it, their lives had not been the same since. In fact, he said, they thought it was one of the best books—besides the Bible—they had ever read.

Before I knew what I was doing, I hugged them both! Then hurrying down the long corridor to the gate where my plane was waiting, I suddenly realized—*Praise the Lord!*—how badly I had misjudged that fine, intelligent couple! *Thank You, Jeeesus!* They may have been a little gabby, but—*Hallelujah!*—nobody's per-fect! I decided right then and there—*Glory be to God!*—that su-persaints aren't so bad after all. At least *Bless God!* that's the way I see it.

32

The Spring That Fed Cedar Park Pool

O God, you are my God, earnestly I seek you; my soul
thirsts for you, my body longs for you, in a dry and weary
land where there is no water.   Psalm 63:1

The Bible has hundreds of verses indicating the importance of
water. It speaks repeatedly of cisterns, springs, wells, rivers, and
brooks. Abraham's servant found a wife for Isaac at the well outside the town of Nahor (Genesis 24:10–26), and Isaac reopened
the wells his father Abraham had dug (Genesis 26:18). Moses
met his wife Zipporah beside a well in Midian (Exodus 2:15).
When David was battling the Philistines he "longed for water
from the well at Bethlehem," and three of his mighty men broke
through the Philistine lines to get it for him (1 Chronicles
11:15–20). That same well is a source of water for Bethlehem
today. In a semi-arid land like Israel, no natural provision was
more important than a reliable source of pure water.

In Numbers 20 when the children of Israel complained for

lack of water at the Desert of Zin, God provided miraculous water out of the rock. In 1 Corinthians 10:4, Paul says, "And that rock was Christ."

Just as a reliable source of pure water is needed to sustain life in the natural realm, so are streams and rivers of living water needed to sustain life in the Spirit. It is no wonder, then, that after asking the woman at the well of Samaria for a drink of water, Jesus added:

> "Everyone who drinks this water will be thirsty again, but whoever drinks the water I give him will never thirst. Indeed, the water I give him will become in him a spring of water welling up to eternal life."   John 4:13–14

But it is not Jesus, the Water of Life, who is stirring up trouble today so much as it is Jesus who baptizes in the Holy Spirit.

> On the last and greatest day of the Feast, Jesus stood and said in a loud voice, "If a man is thirsty, let him come to me and drink. Whoever believes in me, as the Scripture has said, streams of living water will flow from within him." By this he meant the Spirit, whom those who believed in him were later to receive [at Pentecost]. Up to that time the Spirit had not been given, since Jesus had not yet been glorified.   John 7:37–39

The problem is that believers in too many churches have lived in spiritually dry places for so long that they have no real conception of the miraculous difference those "streams of living water" can make. In fact, they see such an unexpected resource as a threat rather than a blessing. I remember a couple of churches in my hometown that had a problem like that.

Wichita Falls, Texas, where I grew up, once had the reputation for having "the world's worst water." Even when I was a small boy, our family bought spring water for drinking purposes, five gallons at a time, in big glass bottles—twenty-five cents and bring your own bottle. Not only that, July and August temperatures in Texas regularly exceed 100 degrees. Believe me, that kind of temperature makes you appreciate cold spring water.

Another blessing for us was the fact that just a mile down the street from our house, beyond the last row of houses and tucked away in a grove of trees, was Cedar Park swimming pool, which water came from a fresh cold spring located right on the park property.

Almost every day during the summer, my two brothers and I would hike that mile barefooted to go swimming in water colder and fresher than the water in any other pool in town. I remember there was a large standpipe about three inches in diameter coming up out of the ground beside the pool from which spring water gushed in a constant stream. Everyone who swam in the pool also took long refreshing drinks from that pipe. I can recall the taste of that cold spring water even today.

Some twenty years after I had grown up and moved away, Cedar Park closed. The swimming pool and buildings around it were razed and the land sold to a developer. Still later, a large downtown denominational church bought the acreage where the pool had been located, planning to build a new church.

But when excavation for the basement of the new church began, they struck the same spring that had provided water for Cedar Park pool. Only this time, that pure spring water was considered a bane rather than a blessing. Since the building contractor found it impossible to completely seal off the flow of water, the trustees of the church called an emergency meeting to consider what to do about the unwanted spring. Some enthusiastic members recommended that it be channeled into a fountain and reflecting pool, and the architecture of the church changed to accommodate the unexpected resource. But more conservative heads prevailed and it was decided—despite the added cost—to fill in the excavation and abandon the project. The church purchased property next to the original site and proceeded to build there, hopefully far enough away that no spring of living water would ever again endanger their church.

Then they sold the first property to another developer who in turn sold it to a church of a different denomination. Aware of the water problems, the new owners avoided excavating deeply and carefully erected a new church building on the property without disturbing the spring.

When I learned what had happened, I couldn't help wondering if there were not at least a few people in those two churches who might have seen some spiritual significance in the events that took place.

For me, the story of the spring that fed Cedar Park pool contains all the ironies of a modern parable, exemplifying all those ministers and churches today who still reject the current outpouring of the Holy Spirit; who are still trying desperately to avoid getting wet from springs of living water with which God is blessing His people. They continue to identify each new spring as a threat, going to great lengths to seal off and bury its flow, determined to prevent their people from partaking of its precious life-giving benefits.

I don't hear much from my hometown these days. All in my family have long since died or moved away, so I haven't heard any recent news concerning either the church that fled from the spring or the one that built right over it but managed to avoid releasing its waters.

I suppose any church, if it tries hard enough, can prevent fresh water from interfering with its plans and programs. But only for a season. In the end, Jesus, the Baptizer in the Holy Spirit, will see to it that the whole Body of Christ is blessed by those springs of living water He promised.

33

Seventeen Faces, All of Them Me

Recently I spent several nights in a hotel room with an over-abundance of mirrors. Even the folding doors of the closet were mirrored so that when I pulled them open, I not only saw myself in each one, but in reflections of reflections I also saw both my left and my right profile.

Then I recalled how—as a boy of twelve—I discovered I had a knack for sketching profiles. I drew profile portraits of my father, my mother, my brothers Hal and Fred, my cousin Corky, and my bird dog, Penny. The portraits actually resembled their subjects, except they all looked rather stiff and solemn. Even Penny, who never had a solemn day in her life.

My great frustration was that I could not draw a self-portrait. Not because I didn't want to, but because I had never seen my own face in profile, although, goodness knows, I had tried often enough! I can't count the times I stood sideways in front of a mirror, rolling my eyes to one side—trying to see the side of my face without turning my head—until my eyes blurred and I got a stiff neck.

Then one day, holding a hand mirror at a certain angle while standing before another mirror, I glimpsed my profile for the very first time. At last, I saw a face that others had always known me by, but I had never seen.

In that hotel room, not only were the closet doors mirrored; mirrors also covered three walls of the bathroom. In the one over the sink I saw the same image I always see when I wash my face. But in the mirrors on either side, my face peered out of multiplied reflections that repeated themselves into the distance as if they might go on forever. Wondering just how many I could see, I leaned forward until I could count eight faces in each direction before bumping my head against the glass.

So, I had to settle for seventeen faces; one in the middle, eight to each side. If you had been standing where I was, you could have seen seventeen reflections of your own face as well.

The truth is, each of us carries around some extra faces. Some, like our profiles, are invisible to us but easily recognized by everyone else. Others we deliberately put on to conceal what we are really like.

Faces in mirrors never change but the real faces we wear vary greatly. Yet even they seldom reveal us as we really are, what we really think or how we really feel. Our best faces may fool the public or even our friends, but not one of them fools God. "The Lord said to Samuel, . . . 'Man looks at the outward appearance, but the Lord looks at the heart' " (1 Samuel 16:7). And faces are part of our outward appearance.

> Seventeen faces, all of them me.
> How many more does my Father see?
>
> How many faces do You see,
> Father God, when You look at me?
> My hopeful face, my fearful face?
> My lonely or my tearful face?
> The modest face, which covers my pride?
> The honest face, which denies I lied?
> The face that turns away from You?

The face that hides my sin from view?
The pleading face that no one sees
When I ask forgiveness on my knees?

Seventeen faces, all of them me.
How many more does my Father see?

I find that the older I get, the easier it becomes to hide behind those different faces, and that's unfortunate. The Bible extols the virtue of having a "single eye," but surely it's just as important to cultivate a single face, "an open countenance."

We most often identify people by faces, but first impressions are not always accurate. All of us have met folks who appeared beautiful or handsome at first. But after getting to know them we find they are not so attractive after all. "How could I ever have thought of him as handsome, or her as beautiful?" we mutter, and quote old slogans to ourselves like, "Pretty is as pretty does."

Perhaps the best thing to remember in all this talk about mirrors and faces is that for Christians hoping to be transformed daily into Jesus' likeness, the Father sees the job already done. Looking at us, He sees only the face of His Son because we are "hid with Christ in God" (Colossians 3:3, KJV).

Time passes while God proves His faithfulness. Our years of beholding His glory follow one after another until the days we make the glad discovery that grace once only *imputed,* has at last been *imparted* and we have become what we beheld.

But we all, with open face beholding as in a [mirror] the glory of the Lord, are changed into the same image from glory to glory.   2 Corinthians 3:18, KJV

What a wonderful promise to keep in mind, each time we gaze in the mirror.

34

Prophecy Fulfilled

Lord, you have been our dwelling place throughout all
generations. . . . A thousand years in your sight are like a
day that has just gone by, or like a watch in the night.

Psalm 90:1, 4

I remember the summer when I was twelve years old and in a
hurry to grow up—August days in Texas were long and sizzling
hot and there wasn't much to do except try to stay cool—complaining to my mother about how slowly the days seemed to pass.
She smiled and said, "Son, the days seem to go slow only because
you are so young. Just wait." Then she quoted what my great-
grandmother Curtsinger, who lived to be eighty-three, used to
say about time going faster the older you get. "The first ten
years crawl, the second ten years walk, the third ten years run—
and after that they fly."

Those words were hard to believe then, but now that I'm in
my sixty-first year I find myself in complete agreement with
Granny Curtsinger. How the years have flown! How could I
have reached and passed my sixtieth birthday so quickly? And
when Alice and I visit our grandchildren, I shake my head and

say, "It seems only yesterday that our children—their parents—were that size!"

But as David said, God's perspective on time varies greatly from our own. To Him "a thousand years are like a day that has just gone by." The older I become, the more I can see why the Bible sometimes describes the passing of a whole generation with a single sentence or paragraph. It's because God patiently begins projects that may take years or decades or even centuries to complete.

We're the ones who are impatient. We desire to see things happen now, today, right this minute! We want results in a hurry. That's because we ourselves are almost always in a hurry. And the younger we are, the bigger the hurry we are in. If you doubt that, just watch how teenagers drive in traffic!

But a very special blessing can attend the passing of our decades. We may live to see the day when seeds sown years before reach maturity and begin bearing their own good fruit.

Recently, Bob Mumford, Charles Simpson, and I attended the annual National Religious Broadcasters Convention in Washington, D.C. During those few days, many people stopped at our booth to express appreciation for our ministries. One man, now a vice-president of a Christian television network, told me how a message on spiritual welfare that I had given over ten years ago had changed his life. Another couple, now operating a Christian radio station, shared how they received the baptism in the Holy Spirit in 1971 while reading a book of mine. Other people shared similar testimonies with Bob and Charles.

It is a deeply moving experience to hear how something you taught or wrote ten, fifteen, or even twenty years ago changed the life of someone who today is exercising his own mature ministry. The passing of the years makes you more and more grateful for the faithfulness of God.

To explain the most gratifying thing that happened to me during the convention, I must go back to Bible-college days at Phillips University in Enid, Oklahoma. While I was still in undergraduate school, Alice and I began a small charismatic prayer group in our home and a number of other student ministers and their wives began to attend. Healings, visions, prophecies, and other supernatural manifestations of the Holy Spirit took place in our meetings. I recorded the controversial effects of that small Pentecostal visitation at Phillips University in a chapter of my first book, *Face Up with a Miracle.* In that chapter, I described one particular girl, Joanne, who—at the urging of the college president's wife—attended our meeting for just one evening. She was greatly blessed by God, but refused to become a part of the group for fear of being criticized. In my book, I summarized her visit this way:

> One girl came and sat quietly through an evening with us. During the meeting tears came to her eyes as she testified to an overwhelming awareness of the love of God. But when I saw her the next day on campus, her defenses were up. "I appreciate being invited to your meeting," she said, "and I'm convinced that what happens there is wholly of God. But you're playing with dynamite and I don't want to get involved."[1]

What that brief summary did not include was that Joanne also received the baptism of the Holy Spirit that night. In addition, I was given a prophetic word that in time she would be used in a significant ministry.

Back then, of course, we were still new and inexperienced in the move of the Spirit, so her refusal to join our group made me wonder if her baptism in the Holy Spirit was real, or if the prophecy I had spoken over her was valid.

The prayer meeting Joanne attended was held on an April evening in 1954. At the National Religious Broadcasters Convention in Washington, D.C., in January 1986, thirty-two years later, I was standing at our booth when a woman who looked

---

[1] *Face Up with a Miracle,* Whitaker House, Greensburg, Pa., 1967, p. 70.

vaguely familiar approached me, hands extended. Her face broke into a broad smile as she spoke my name. Then I recognized her—it was Joanne!

She shared briefly how she had married after college and how she and her husband had followed careers in Christian music for nearly thirty years. Then, just two years previously, they had set aside those careers to begin what was proving to be a fruitful ministry to homosexuals in the city of New York.

"I'll never forget the prayer meeting when you and your wife prayed for me," Joanne said. "I want you to know that even though I tried to reject what God did for me, I really did receive the Holy Spirit that night and the prophecy you spoke over me is finally being fulfilled."

Some of you reading these words may be discouraged because your present life doesn't seem to be producing much fruit for the Kingdom of God. But fruit takes time to produce, and God's perspective about time is different from our own. Our task is to go on sowing; in God's own time, there will be a harvest.

After a year? After ten years? After thirty-two years? What does it matter when God has all eternity to work in?

— 35

Believe in Your Calling

Let every man abide in the same calling wherein he was
called.   1 Corinthians 7:20, KJV

At times, nothing helps to keep us going more than believing
we have been called by God to do what we are doing. Then, even
insignificant tasks can take on grandeur because we feel we're
part of God's overall purpose.

A story is told about Sir Christopher Wren, the famous archi-
tect who designed some of England's grandest cathedrals. One
day while visiting a construction site he found three men toiling
in an excavation.

"What are you men doing?" Sir Christopher asked.

"I'm just shoveling dirt," one replied sourly.

"I'm just digging a ditch," the second man complained.

But the third man responded with pride, "I'm helping Sir
Christopher Wren build a great cathedral."

Unfortunately, many Christians downgrade the significance of
their calling and the value of their contribution to the Kingdom
of God, simply because they are not preachers or evangelists or

missionaries. They have bought the devil's lie that work must be religious to be sacred.

But in God's sight, any task is sacred if it is performed well and performed to His glory. Moreover, God has called millions of believers to perform a whole host of significant tasks that will never be identified as "religious," but are as necessary to the ongoing work of the Kingdom of God as preaching, praying, or prophesying. And it is a marvelous thing to watch a man doing the work he knows God has called him to do, even if others may consider his job "unspiritual."

Some time ago, when Alice and I were returning home from a Bible seminar in another state, we stopped at a modest little diner for lunch, not knowing we were about to spend an amazing thirty minutes in a cheerful outpost of the Kingdom of God.

The diner's owner and chef, a wiry, baldheaded little man with a smile as broad as all outdoors, was positioned behind the grill so that he could benevolently survey all the patrons in his restaurant. As we entered he greeted us with a warm, "You folks come right on in!"

We sat in a booth by the window and with increasing admiration and awe, watched that little chef fry and serve hamburgers to the glory of God. If ever a man had found his calling, he had. Grace flowed through every motion as he lifted his spatula to flip and flatten each beef patty browning on the grill at exactly the right moment.

He sliced the buns and applied mustard and ketchup with the confident flourish of a great symphony director and, with fingers nimble and talented as those of a concert pianist, arranged the lettuce, the pickle, and the onion slices on each one. All this took place under the canopy of a beaming smile, accompanied by cheerful, uplifting banter with the customers, while two attractive teenaged daughters served the orders with sunny efficiency.

Everyone in the restaurant could tell that happy little cook not only loved frying hamburgers, he loved making people feel good watching him fry them and feel even better when they ate them.

Totally devoid of platitudes, his was a simple gospel of loving service, which blessed everyone fortunate enough to enter his diner.

Alice and I ate our hamburgers with thanksgiving and left the little restaurant nourished in spirit as well as body, wishing fervently that the grace and confidence that motivated that humble chef could become the portion of every frustrated believer who blunders his way through life feeling like a second-rate Christian because he "has no ministry."

How do you feel about your present placement in the Body of Christ? Are you an engineer, a teacher, a carpenter, a secretary? Are you a homemaker, a mechanic, a musician, a salesman? An electrician, a plumber, a student, or a stockbroker? Then thank God He's called you to do what you are doing and don't belittle your place in His scheme of things! In Jesus' day, priests were so plentiful they had to cast lots to see who could have Temple duty (see Luke 1:8–10). But when He chose His twelve disciples, Jesus preferred fishermen and tax collectors. There was not a priest in the whole bunch!

So whatever your work is, take pride in it. In God's eyes, your place in His plan and your task in the Kingdom are just as important as anyone's.

Family Honor

Therefore God exalted him to the highest place and gave
him the name that is above every name.

Philippians 2:9

Children born into an honored, wealthy family are entitled to
all the rights and privileges of that family. To be born into the
Christian family is to gain full access to the privileges and benefits of the family name. Jesus tells us that whatever we need we
are to ask for—not in our own name—but in His (John 14:13).

The privilege of praying in His name should be a constant,
humbling reminder to us that grace has been given—not because
our name is worthy—but because *His* name is worthy and because He has made us part of His family. It is often much easier,
however, to accept the rights and privileges than the responsibilities of bearing His name.

When we were growing up, my parents repeatedly drilled into
me and my two brothers the importance of honoring the family name. "Don't do anything that will dishonor the name of
Basham," they said. And when we did sometimes misbehave
in public, they would scold or spank us with the reminder,

"Bashams just don't behave like that!" So I grew up knowing that I must live a life worthy of the Basham name.

In time, my wife and I taught the same principle to our children, who are also teaching their children the meaning of family honor. I trust most of you who are parents are doing the same thing.

Recently, I had an experience that reminded me all over again of my parents' admonition. While I was ministering in a western city, friends took my wife and me to dinner at an exclusive country club. We were waiting for our table when I noticed an announcement on a bulletin board listing club members who had been suspended for failure to pay their club charges. Not only were their names listed, but the amount of their debts as well. Casually looking at the list, I was suddenly stunned to see my name, Don Basham, listed as a suspended member! Moreover, it said I owed the club $1,113.67!

I cannot describe the emotional turmoil of the next ninety seconds. Even though I knew the name on the list was some other Don Basham, I struggled against rising feelings of shame and embarrassment as a parental admonition fifty years old echoed inside: "Bashams don't behave like that!"

For three days I had been the guest speaker at a church in the city with radio and newspapers advertising the meetings. What if someone dining at the club heard my name on the radio or had attended the meetings and then saw that name on the bulletin board and thought it meant me?

I had to resist a panicky impulse to tear the sheet from the bulletin board before anyone else could read it. After all, it was not as if my name were Bill Smith or John Brown. How many Don Bashams could there be?

I tried to joke about the matter with my hosts, but as we sat at our table I kept glancing around the dining room to see if anyone was staring at me. For hours afterward I continued to feel a certain indignation over my name being posted in public as a person who was financially irresponsible. And I was angry with the real culprit for dragging "our" name through the mud. Anyone bearing my name, I thought, should have more respect for it.

Then I made the mistake of complaining to God. I said silently, "God, I'm in this city as Your representative. Don't You care about my reputation?" The thought that immediately came to mind was both quick and unsettling. "Do you care about *My* reputation when *My* name is dragged through the mud by those who bear it?"

Then I began to recall the many times I have acted in selfish ways that dishonored the name of Jesus. I found myself quickly apologizing. "Lord, please forgive me for all those things I have said and done that have brought reproach upon Your name."

But God was not ready to let me off the hook. "I'm also concerned about that other Don Basham," he seemed to say, implying I was not.

He was right. Concerned about my own reputation, I hadn't even considered there might be valid reasons why the other Don Basham had failed to pay his debts to the club. Then I remembered that certain industries in that city had recently fallen on hard times and that employment for many professionals had been terminated. It was quite probable, even likely, that my counterpart was an honest but recently unemployed executive facing economic hardship far beyond the debts that barred him from the premises of the club, while I sat there basking in both the spiritual and material blessings of God.

So I had to ask forgiveness a second time. This time I said, "Lord, I also ask You to forgive me for judging the brother who bears my name. Will You please bless him and his family and let them begin to experience the same abundant grace with which You have blessed me and my family."

Then I filed for future reference another significant spiritual lesson, with the fervent hope that the Lord would take note of my renewed resolve to show more concern for His name and reputation than my own.

Church and Clergy Foibles:
Part 1

foible: a minor flaw or shortcoming in personal character or behavior

Paul was right, of course, when he wrote in 1 Corinthians 1:21 (KJV) how ". . . it pleased God by the foolishness of preaching to save them that believe." But while the Kingdom of God advances through the foolishness of preaching, it can suffer setbacks through the foolishness of preachers. Paul also wrote:

But we have this treasure in earthen vessels, that the surpassing greatness of the power may be of God and not from ourselves.   2 Corinthians 4:7, NAS

Sometimes we "earthen vessels" say and do some strange things in the name of the Lord. In fact, some of the things even supposedly mature Christians say and do, believing they are serving the Lord, not only boggle the mind, they actually frustrate the purposes of God.

During my years as a minister in the Christian Church—a denomination that practices believer baptism by immersion—there was a raging controversy over whether or not our congregations should accept Christians from non-immersionist churches into full membership without requiring them to be rebaptized. Liberal churches in the denomination felt accepting the new members promoted church unity; conservative churches believed it was heresy.

While I was still in seminary and preaching on weekends in a rural church in southern Oklahoma, a small Christian church in a nearby town planned a congregational meeting after its Sunday service to vote on changing from a "closed membership" church to an "open membership" church.

The minister and elders of a conservative "closed membership" church a few miles away learned of the congregational meeting and devised a plan to prevent their sister church from falling into heresy. On the day of the meeting, the "closed membership" church canceled its own service and the entire congregation of some sixty-five members drove fifteen miles to attend services at the other church. To the embarrassment of the pastor, when he gave the usual invitation to join the church at the end of the service, the minister and every member of the visiting congregation came forward to transfer their membership, thus becoming eligible to vote in the congregational meeting that followed. Their votes carried the election and the terrible heresy of "open membership" was defeated. The following Sunday, in the full flush of victory, all the members transferred their membership back to their own church, fully convinced that a telling blow had been struck in behalf of theological orthodoxy!

If we disregard the ethics of such behavior one might say their action did make some kind of theological statement. On the other hand, if they intended to effect any lasting change in the life of the other congregation by such a crude and unloving action, they were sadly mistaken. The hollowness of the victory became apparent when the church they joined for just one week held another congregational meeting two weeks later and voted in "open membership" anyway.

The point is, even the most noble spiritual objectives can never justify radical and foolhardy actions. How greatly we all need to understand that rather than the ends *justifying* the means, the means *determine* the ends. And that same principle applies not only to our deeds but our words as well. Nevertheless, enthusiastic, overzealous believers never seem to tire in their attempts to advance the Kingdom of God by ill-advised shortcuts or alterations.

I recently received through the mail an announcement concerning the publication of a new gospel. Not a new translation; *a new gospel!* The brochure described the new Bible as presenting Christ "the way He really was." It claimed the authors of the original Gospels "inserted their sinful selves" into their work and presented Jesus as "sometimes divine, and sometimes . . . a sinner." However, this new gospel—"written under the influence, direction, and power of the Holy Spirit"—was described as portraying "a better, more divine Jesus than the original four Gospels do." The author then modestly listed ten reasons why his new and improved gospel would be "a tremendous help to the cause of Christianity."

Acknowledging the author's academic credentials—an ordained minister with earned degrees from two major U.S. universities and one major seminary—I nevertheless longed to ask him why the Holy Spirit waited so many centuries to confess that He had bungled the job with Matthew, Mark, Luke, and John so badly that a new version of the Gospel was needed to set the record straight.

I was about to write him when the Holy Spirit gently reminded me that most believers are guilty of the same sin. According to the portions of Scripture we accept and the portions we reject, we also regularly rewrite the Gospel to suit ourselves. We love its promises; we avoid its disciplines. We embrace those teachings that confirm our convictions and dismiss those that don't as "not meant for today." We bask in Gospel blessings, but shun Gospel commitment. We cherish our own peculiar doctrines, while blithely condemning the convictions of other men for whom Christ died.

I decided not to write the letter.

It remains to be seen if that ambitious minister's "new gospel" will find a significant readership. Somehow, I rather doubt it. I suspect it will be no more effective than the act of that conservative church that transferred its entire membership for one week, just to steal an election.

Personally, I've never been tempted to actually write a new Bible; I've enough trouble being accountable for certain books, sermons, and Bible studies I've already produced, not to mention all the unscriptural things I've said and done.

Lord, I want to thank You for Your patience in putting up with all the impulsive, unwise, and unloving things we do and say in our attempts to serve You. Without Your forbearance, we'd all be in big trouble.

38

Church and Clergy Foibles: Part 2

Don't let anyone look down on you because you are young, but set an example for the believers in speech, in life, in love, in faith and in purity.   1 Timothy 4:12

I suspect one reason Paul had to advise Timothy in such a manner was because some older members of the congregation he was serving doubted whether one so young could do the job. Paul, who was discipling Timothy in his ministry by letter and by personal visits, urged him to begin by setting the right example, both in personal behavior and in the content of his teaching. Paul already knew what Timothy was still destined to learn, that spiritual maturity is a matter of very slow growth from very small beginnings. As our Lord explained it:

". . . So is the kingdom of God, as if a man should cast seed into the ground [and] . . . the earth bringeth forth fruit of

herself; *first the blade, then the ear, after that the full corn in
the ear.*"   Mark 4:26–28, KJV, italics added

Early on, I discovered what amazing patience God can show
toward young, immature preachers who say and do weird, immature things while attempting to minister His Word. Like most
young men training for the ministry, I did my first preaching
during Bible-college days.

My alma mater, Phillips University and its Graduate Seminary
in Enid, Oklahoma, provided pulpit ministry for approximately
140 small rural churches in a 250-mile radius across Oklahoma
and parts of southern Kansas and north Texas. Arrangements
were made like this: A pulpit committee from the church would
contact the director of ministries at the Bible college, who then
sent a prospective student minister to the church for a trial sermon. If the congregation found the young man acceptable, he
would serve the church as weekend pastor for two or three years,
until he graduated or accepted ministry at another church closer
to the Bible college.

For ministerial students it provided both a chance to gain
preaching experience and part-time employment. For small
churches unable to afford a full-time minister it was an economic
necessity. Spiritually, however, it was risky as Russian roulette,
since student ministers—while spiritually immature—often show
a frightening capability for conjuring up novel, even bizarre ways
of presenting the Gospel. One student, brimming with overcon-
fidence, set out to prove his spiritual wisdom to his small congregation on his very first Sunday. The title of his sermon was
"Jesus' Fifteen Mistakes."

Yet another classmate revealed how he planned to instill fresh
motivation in his complacent congregation. We listened and then
strongly suggested to him that delivering a sermon while dressed
like the devil—complete with red costume and cap with horns—

might not be the best way to motivate a small, conservative farm congregation. He dismissed our reservations with a wave of the hand and proceeded with his plan. Apparently his sermon did instill some fresh motivation for the congregation; immediately after the service they voted unanimously to fire him.

Through succeeding centuries the church has had to endure the limitations of young men called of God to serve His Church because, unfortunately, spiritual wisdom and maturity do not automatically accompany the call. Church history relates how a young Anglican priest stubbornly refused to serve Holy Communion to a young woman he desired to court, simply because she spurned his affections for those of another man. But John Wesley outgrew his youthful petulance eventually to become England's greatest evangelist and the founder of Methodism.

Even Jesus grew in the understanding of His Messiahship through experience. "Although he was a son, *he learned obedience* from what he suffered" (Hebrews 5:8, italics added).

While my own days as a student minister were not marked by any major crisis brought on by my ministerial inexpertise—at least, not that I remember—I do recall preaching any number of lame, inane, inadequate, and sometimes mercifully short messages in the three student pastorates I served during my undergraduate and my seminary years.

Today, I pay tribute to whatever saints may still remain in those small churches: the patient saints in the Christian churches in Burkburnett, Texas; Howard, Kansas; and Ft. Cobb, Oklahoma. They survived the enthusiasms of a young green preacher preaching young green sermons, yet did not "look down on him because he was young." Without realizing it, they helped the Holy Spirit preserve and nourish one more weak and unlikely "blade" that could one day blossom into "a full ear of corn."

The way I see it, without their loving acceptance and encouragement—and that of many more saints just like them—my contribution to the Kingdom of God would have ended almost before it began.

39

Church and Clergy Foibles: Part 3

You then, my son, be strong in the grace that is in Christ
Jesus.   2 Timothy 2:1

As we have already noted, Paul had many significant things to
say to young Timothy concerning the problems he encountered
in the exercise of his ministry. Of course, every new generation
of ministers faces its own set of challenges and problems. For
young ministers today, who have only the benefit of Paul's letters
and not his personal oversight, one major challenge consists of
simply surviving seminary training and the various traumatic experiences encountered in learning how to preach and pastor a
church.

Statistically, the mortality rate is high among potential men of
the cloth. Long before completing their training, many become
disillusioned and discouraged, not only with the theological ab-
stractions that fill so many seminary courses, but also with the
spiritual apathy of the small congregations on which they cut

their preaching teeth. In frustration they turn to other, less demanding, and more lucrative professions.

In the two previous chapters, I listed some of the strange things the Lord and His Church endure as a result of the unpredictable activities of young men training for the ministry. But it's not just young preachers who come up with strange ideas about how the Church and the Kingdom of God should function; the churches they serve have equally strange ideas. ⹀

One of my seminary classmates—usually a cheerful, confident young man—returned from his pastorate late one Sunday night, wearing a very long face. When some of us tried to find out why he was depressed, he finally admitted he had lost his job. Further inquiry revealed he had been sacked, not because the members of his church were dissatisfied with his preaching, but because they wanted to carpet the church sanctuary. Since the weekly church offerings would not bring in enough money both to pay the preacher and buy the carpet, they fired the preacher.

For the next nine months the enterprising congregation held Sunday services without a minister, using his salary for carpet payments. Once the new carpet was fully paid for, the pulpit committee returned to the Bible college to see if their former preacher was still available, only to learn he had been hired by another church that didn't need a carpet. So the director of ministerial services—after being assured the church had no further plans for renovating their building—sent them a different student pastor.

Another student minister was so successful in winning new members to his church that the elders decided they could afford a full-time minister. The unemployed minister they hired agreed to begin his duties in two weeks but no one had the courage to tell the student pastor that his days were numbered. The elders finally decided to break the news by adding one more announcement to the list regularly left for the minister to read from the pulpit. So during the service the following Sunday morning, the young minister not only informed the church that Thursday night choir practice would be held as usual, but also that a new minister had been hired and would assume his duties the following week. Then pausing to ponder what he had just read, he added, "I suppose that means I've been fired."

He was correct.

But even with a student minister trying his best and the congregation wanting to cooperate, there were still unexpected challenges. My first student pastorate was at Burkburnett, Texas, a long 210 miles from Bible school. The drafty little building had a low ceiling that during the winter months trapped the heat from the gas stove. The pulpit was located on a two-foot-high platform at one end of the room. On cold mornings, comfortable temperature for the congregation meant hot, uncomfortable temperature above the pulpit. Every Sunday from November to March, when I stood up to preach it was like placing my head inside an oven.

Describing my dilemma privately to the chairman of the board of elders, I hinted that turning the heat down just a little could greatly improve my lot in life. He listened sympathetically, then said, "But you wouldn't want the old folks listening to your sermons to get cold, now would you?"

So during the winter months I tried to see my weekly hot head, my weekly headaches, my weekly dry throat and stuffed-up sinuses as sacrifices to God and the Christian ministry. As Alice observed, brave missionaries on foreign fields endured much more. "I know it's uncomfortable for you when you stand up to preach, dear," she said sweetly, "but it still beats traveling up the Amazon in a leaky boat."

On really cold days, the warm temperature in the little sanctuary proved irresistible for some of the men used to working in the cold out-of-doors. Still, I never quite got used to watching grown men fall asleep while I tried to preach.

But at least I was spared the lot of my successor, a classmate named Kenneth. Hired by the church after I secured a pastorate closer to school, he was also destined to face the double peril of stuffed-up sinuses and dozing deacons. Kenneth's very first Sunday at the church came on a cold January day. In the overheated sanctuary, the chairman of the board of deacons fell asleep early in the service. His wife ignored her slumbering husband until Kenneth stood up to preach. Then she elbowed him sharply, so he wouldn't miss the new pastor's first sermon.

The deacon came awake mumbling aloud and noticed that both the preacher and the congregation were staring at him. In his confused state of mind—he later reported—he thought the service had ended and the new pastor had called upon him to announce the benediction, a duty it regularly fell his lot to perform.

So just as Kenneth opened his mouth to begin his first sermon in his new church, the chairman of the board of deacons solemnly rose to his feet and began to pray aloud.

"Dismiss us now, O Lord, with your blessing. . . ."

It was probably more a conditioned reflex than anything else that led almost half the congregation to rise to their feet and start toward the door.

In the class the following week, Kenneth complained to me what a terribly embarrassing incident it had been for him, for the deacon, for the deacon's wife, and for the whole congregation, and how awful it had been for a thing like that to happen on his very first Sunday at the church.

"That's too bad, Kenneth," I tried to console him. "But just remember that preaching in that stuffy little church still beats traveling up the Amazon in a leaky boat."

40

Immediate Retribution

Let every person be in subjection to the governing authorities. *For there is no authority except from God,* and those which exist are established by God. Therefore he who resists authority has opposed the ordinance of God; and they who have opposed will receive condemnation upon themselves.   Romans 13:1–2, NAS, italics added

Most of us forget that on earth God delegates His authority to others. Moreover, we find it easy to disobey some delegated authorities since punishment for our disobedience is often delayed. Scripture does say the Lord is "slow to anger, abounding in love" (Psalm 103:8), but it also says He "will not leave the guilty unpunished" (Nahum 1:3).

In fact, God can judge man's rebellion instantly if He decides to, and I have vivid memories of one occasion when He did just that. It happened a long time ago and it taught me a sober lesson about obeying delegated authority.

Every year when the spring rains came, the water level in our city lake would rise and pour over a six-foot-high spillway into the creek below. When that happened, fishing just below the spillway became excellent, and weekends would find dozens of local fishermen—often including my dad and me—lining the banks of the creek.

The best fishing spot was the center of the concrete apron extending along the base of the spillway where a fisherman had ideal access to the huge pool below. That is, if fishing had been allowed there. Unfortunately, a big sign posted on the bank read, "No Fishing from the Spillway!"

As a frustrated fourteen-year-old fisherman, I was about to disregard the sign one day, until my father stopped me. "It's against the law, son," was his quiet comment when he saw me edging toward the spillway.

My frustration increased when a big burly fellow standing nearby rolled up his trousers and waded rebelliously out onto the spillway apron and immediately began catching fish.

But frustration was forgotten when—on that sunny Saturday afternoon in May of 1940, at the spillway dividing Lake Wichita and Holiday Creek—God decreed swift and solemn judgment upon one who chose to disregard His delegated authority.

Retribution came in the form of a seven-foot-long garter snake, which unsuccessfully attempted to cross the lake just above the spillway. The rebel who didn't believe in signs was standing in ten inches of rushing water with his back to the spillway, when the snake swept over the falls to strike his bare legs from behind.

That the huge serpent suddenly thrashing and coiling around his legs was a non-poisonous, harmless variety, was a zoological fact totally beyond assimilation in the mind of that terrified fisherman. With one agonizing shriek he climbed at least four feet straight up in the air as fishing rod, bait bucket, and string of fish went flying in all directions.

The snake swept swiftly on downstream, head high and slithering furiously as fishermen on both sides of the creek dropped their rods and followed it, shouting and throwing rocks.

The airborne fisherman landed with both legs churning, and in a magnificent effort matching the miracle of Peter walking on water, he covered the entire thirty feet to the bank in three giant strides. Wild-eyed and gasping, he collapsed not far from where my father and I stood.

"M-my G-God! D-did y-you s-see t-that?" he stammered, unaware that God not only saw the whole episode, He ordained it!

My father smiled at me. "Now aren't you glad you obeyed the sign?" he said. Suddenly, my whole being was filled with a rare kind of thanksgiving, a gratitude born out of witnessing an awesome judgment that—had it not been for loving parental authority—would have been my own.

We continued to fish Holiday Creek below Lake Wichita through the years, my dad and I. But never again was I tempted to fish from that spillway. In fact, in all the years since, I have seldom felt tempted either to fish, to hunt, to enter, to loiter, to eat, to sit, to walk, to drive, or to park anywhere a sign representing delegated authority says I shouldn't.

Once witnessed, immediate retribution is not easily forgotten.

— 41

Downwind Landings

He makes the clouds his chariot and rides on the wings of
the wind.   Psalm 104:3

In every art and profession there are basic rules to be followed
if one is to be successful. Disobey the rules, and you end up in
trouble.

There is no more basic rule in the art of flying than the one
that says you always take off and land *into the wind.* Even great
aircraft carriers swing around into the wind to launch or land aircraft from their decks.

To the natural mind, a headwind seems to be a hindrance designed to slow us down. Only when we understand the principles
of flight do we see how essential heading into the wind can be
and how dangerous tailwinds are, especially when taking off or
landing.

Some Christians seem to believe the grace of God should always provide a tailwind. They expect to spend their lives traveling downwind, following the path of least resistance. But to be
led by the Spirit of God does not necessarily mean our journeys

will be quick or easy. In fact, my own experience with God indicates that while it may prove more difficult, the Christian life is more stable and rewarding when we live it facing into the wind. Believers seeking to breeze through life riding a tailwind are prime candidates for a crash landing.

In previous chapters I have mentioned how, as a teenager, I learned to fly in a little yellow Piper Cub airplane. Certain experiences as an eighteen-year-old fledgling pilot proved later to have significant spiritual application. Like the time I tried so hard to make a downwind landing.

It was a cloudy afternoon in May 1944, with a strong hint of rain in the air. My instructor gazed carefully at the gathering clouds and gave me permission to fly for thirty minutes, provided I didn't go far from the airport. Assuring him all I wanted to do was shoot a few landings, I took off into air as heavy and smooth as cream.

The traffic pattern around the small airport at the edge of Wichita Falls was similar to those the country over. Take off *into the wind,* climb to six hundred feet, turn ninety degrees to the left and climb to eight hundred feet. Then, another ninety-degree left turn onto the downwind leg. Another left turn into the base leg, you throttle back to 1500 RPMs and begin your descent. Turning onto the final approach, *into the wind,* you line up with the runway, cut the throttle to idling, come in low over the fence and T-hangars at the end of the field, and level off over the end of the runway. Slowly ease back on the stick, raising the nose of the plane until, in three-point position, you lose flying speed just inches above the ground and drop to the runway.

My first three landings went smooth as silk. But the fourth time I entered the traffic pattern, all at once the little plane began to bounce around the darkening sky, buffeted by sharp gusts of wind, and I realized it was time to get my little plane on the ground. Steering through suddenly hostile air, I turned onto the final approach only to pass over the fence and T-hangars at bewildering speed. Overshooting the runway, I shoved the throttle forward and climbed to six hundred feet to go around again.

Heart pounding, I turned onto the final approach a second time. But even with the throttle all the way closed, the little cub sizzled across the boundary of the field like a fighter plane. I was approaching panic when I saw my instructor standing beside the runway, waving his arms wildly, gesturing toward the windsock. One quick look revealed the wind had not only radically increased in velocity, it had changed 180 degrees in direction.

I was trying to land downwind!

Slamming the throttle forward, I climbed once more to six hundred feet, made a quick 180-degree turn back toward the runway, this time heading properly into the wind. Since the Piper Cub had a landing speed of under 40 mph, heading into a wind of over 30 mph put my speed over the ground at less than 10 mph. I bounced to a landing, rolling toward the hangar door, cut the ignition, and jumped out to help my instructor push the plane into the hangar, just as the first blinding sheets of rain swept across the field.

Then I listened sheepishly as he summed up my foolhardiness with a single sentence: "Trying to land with a 35-mph wind at your tail can have a serious effect on your health."

Today, with many a spiritual journey and some extremely rough landings behind me, I find it best to begin and end every spiritual endeavor facing into the wind. It seems so much safer.

42

The Mun Blewdies

There is a strange story in chapter 12 of Judges, which tells how 42,000 Ephraimites lost their lives simply because they couldn't pronounce a certain word correctly. When they were challenged to pronounce the word "Shibboleth," it came out "Sibboleth." Then the Gileadites identified them as their foes and killed them.

It must be especially embarrassing to lose your life just because something you try to say comes out the wrong way.

Of course, today we don't put people to death for getting their words twisted, but sometimes I have felt almost embarrassed to death when what I wanted to say came out sounding not at all like what I had planned.

As a matter of fact, most of us, at one time or another, have suffered from the mysterious disease my family calls the "Mun Blewdies." Let me tell you how we came to name it that.

It all began when my wife and I were young parents with five children to rear, and I was a busy pastor of a denominational church. For any pastor and his family, Sundays are strenuous, demanding days. Consequently, Mondays often bring a big emotional and physical letdown. When they were especially bad, we came to call them "Blue Mondays." Eventually, a really bad time on any day of the week came to be referred to as "a case of the Blue Mondays."

Once when our oldest daughter, Cindi, about twelve at the time, was having such a day, she identified it with tongue twisting eloquence. "I'm just having a bad case of the Mun Blewdies," she said. Later, when we could stop laughing long enough to ask her if she felt she had recovered, her answer proved she had not. "I think I'm befinning to geel better," she said.

And so was born our name for a mysterious malady that may strike anyone at any time. When it does, it can reduce the most dignified and eloquent speaker to a blithering idiot in a matter of seconds.

The most famous case of the disease on record occurred many years ago, so they tell me, when the President of the United States, Herbert Hoover, was being introduced on nationwide radio. It went something like this:

"And now, ladies and gentlemen," the announcer gravely intoned, "it is my great pleasure to introduce to you, the President of the United States, the Honorable Hervert Hoober."

They say there was a long pause before the announcer valiantly tried to redeem himself. "I beg your pardon, I meant to say, the Honorable Hoobert Herver." That attempt was followed by a hysterical giggle and two more desperate but equally futile efforts to save the day. "I mean, the Honorable Heevert Hoober—er—Hoovert Heeber."

The announcer finally managed to pronounce the President's name correctly, but by the day's end, it was reported, he had considered resigning his job swearing to seek employment in another profession.

It is a fact not generally known, but every man who makes his living speaking in public faces the constant danger of being stricken by the Mun Blewdies. No one is immune. And the more significant the occasion, the more likely the attack.

I sometimes think the Lord allows the attacks so that we will not "think more highly of ourselves than we ought to think."

One thing for sure, when the Mun Blewdies strike in public, a man invariably steps off the speaker's platform more humble than he stepped on.

I know a minister who was attacked at the beginning of a significant spiritual rally being held on the steps of the capitol building in Sacramento, California. His introductory remarks to the several hundred people in attendance began something like this: "Friends, our hearts are filled with gratitude for the privilege of gathering here today on the states of the step capitol . . . ."

As one who also speaks frequently in public, I have been victimized by the dread disease more than once. I have managed to survive, but with scars—permanent reminders of the public embarrassment that inevitably accompanies such attacks since even the most attentive, approving audience will dissolve into fits of hysterical laughter when the Mun Blewdies strike.

Like the time I was sharing with a large congregation how, in my struggles to sell copies of my first book, I would drag a suitcase full of books from city to city. I didn't think it was all that funny, but the audience roared with laughter. Then I realized I had said I would "drag a book full of suitcases" from city to city!

I had a prolonged attack of Mun Blewdies years ago when I was pastoring in Toronto. In my own defense, let me say on that particular occasion, I caught the disease from a visiting evangelist who was conducting a revival in a large Pentecostal tabernacle near the edge of town. An unlettered preacher from Oklahoma, he would have been truly eloquent had it not been for the Mun Blewdies. The night I heard him, he was preaching from the Book of Deuteronomy. During his sermon he must have called the book by name at least twenty times. Only he didn't pronounce it, Deute-RON-omy. When he said it, it came out Deute-ROM-ony. By the time his sermon was over, I don't think anyone in the whole place could have pronounced the fifth book of the Old Testament correctly. I know I couldn't.

My exposure to the evangelist's case of Mun Blewdies affected me almost immediately. The next Sunday morning during my sermon, I recommended a book by a famous English writer named Leslie Weatherhead. Only I called him Wesley Leatherhead. Things became even worse when I went on to preach from John's gospel about how "Jesus of Nazarus raised Lazereth from the dead." My congregation snickered through the rest of my sermon.

Apparently, the Mun Blewdies create some kind of short circuit in the hookup between brain and mouth, so that no matter how carefully you speak, some of your twords will come out wisted. The problem is, even to write about this curious disease seems to expose one to it.

But God is merciful, and even severe cases of the Mun Blewdies seldom last more than a few days. So if, after reading this, you fink you theel symm of the sumptoms of the Mun Blewdies, please don't panic. That's the very thurst wing you can do. Remember that the templem is only problemary and try to stay calm. Take a dreep beth and count to ten! You'll start to feel better almost before you know it.

— 43

How Many Cats
Are Tied to Your Bedpost?

"You have let go of the commands of God and are holding
on to the traditions of men."   Mark 7:8

When Christians are faced with a choice between religious
tradition and new spiritual experience, more times than not they
choose the tradition over the new experience. Remember how
the scribes and Pharisees were so terribly offended when Jesus
healed the man with a withered hand on the Sabbath?

Then Jesus asked them, "Which is lawful on the Sabbath:
to do good or to do evil, to save life or to kill?" But they
remained silent. He looked around at them in anger and,
deeply distressed at their stubborn hearts, said to the man,
"Stretch out your hand." He stretched it out, and his hand
was completely restored. Then the Pharisees went out and
began to plot with the Herodians how they might kill
Jesus.   Mark 3:4–6

The scribes and Pharisees had long since forsaken their sacred responsibilities as stewards of the commandments of God to create a thousand and one picky rituals and regulations designed to obscure true righteousness and lay impossible burdens upon the common people. Trapped by their own precious traditions, they sought to murder Jesus because keeping those traditions had become much more important than meeting human need.

Properly observed, traditions can enrich our heritage and strengthen our ties with the historic family of God. But held too tightly or too long, they may end up as substitutes for the revelation that first inspired them and stand in the way of the next thing God wants to do.

I once read about an anthropologist who, while studying the religious customs of a primitive South American Indian tribe, discovered a strange tradition. Before they went to worship in the temple, every family in the tribe who had a cat tied it to the bedpost. No one seemed to know why, and nothing in their current religious practice suggested any reason for the strange custom. Nevertheless, all the natives agreed it was very important. "It is part of our sacred tradition," they insisted.

Only after weeks of research did the anthropologist discover how, in earlier times, the Indians had brought fresh fish to the temple and placed them on the altar as an offering to their god. Since the village cats kept jumping on the altar to steal the fish, the priests ordered them to be tied up during temple worship. In later generations the practice of offering sacrificial fish was abandoned in favor of a purer form of worship, but the worshipers kept right on tying their cats to the bedposts.

When God provides fresh revelation, we may have to abandon certain traditions and rituals that no longer contain spiritual reality. Jesus said, "New wine calls for new wineskins" (see Matthew 9:17). But since new wine threatens to burst old wineskins, we often decide to keep the old familiar skins and throw out the new wine.

Even when the new revelation begins to be accepted, some of

the old traditions and rituals it renders obsolete are often maintained, just because "we've always done it that way." We forget that every sacred tradition was first considered the innovation of some heretical nonconformist.

As creatures of habit, Christians tend to be very conservative. That can become a problem since, as one definition points out, "a conservative is one who believes that nothing should ever be done for the first time."

Even after years of ministry to Christians with many differences in doctrine and tradition, I still encounter new and unfamiliar forms of worship and ministry that run roughshod over pet traditions of my own. "That can't be right! I've never seen it done that way before!" I feel like saying—until I see the Holy Spirit blessing His people.

Then I have to repent and ask God's forgiveness, and untie one more cat from my bedpost.

How many cats are tied to your bedpost?

Keep It Simple

And the Lord answered me, and said, Write the vision, and make it plain upon tables [tablets], that he may run that readeth it.   Habakkuk 2:2, KJV

As one who both writes and edits for a living, I am continually aware of how difficult it is to communicate clearly. When I read or try to edit an article that falls short of the literary quality necessary for publication, I recall a line from a popular movie, "What we have here is a failure to communicate."

In his excellent book *The Power of Little Words*, author John Beckley, former business editor of *Newsweek* magazine, observes:

> The emphasis in education is rarely placed on communicating ideas simply and clearly. Instead we're encouraged to use more complicated words and sentence structures to show off our learning and literacy. . . . Instead of teaching us how to communicate as clearly as possible, our schooling in English teaches us how to fog things up. It even implants

a fear that if we don't make our writing complicated enough, we'll be considered uneducated.

The problem we are talking about spills over into practically every kind of writing, all the way from books and magazines down to those little sheets of instruction that accompany kits of things that have to be put together. Have you ever tried to read and follow those dumb instructions? Just the other day my wife brought home a package containing an unassembled frame for drying sweaters. Opening it I found a little slip of paper, which read:

Instructions
Pivot four hinged arms into cross.
Slip single tabbed arm extension into each slotted sleeve, with double tabbed bend pointing upward.
Position nylon corner eyelets over ends of upward arm extensions.
Place plastic tip on wire ends to lock nylon surface.
Place towel under dryer to absorb excess moisture, when not used in tub.

I looked at the pile of strangely bent pieces of wire and single piece of nylon fabric and then again at the sheet of instructions and mumbled to myself, "What we have here is a failure to communicate." Then recalling the Scripture that says, "With God all things are possible," I made a positive confession before I began. Honest I did. But it still took thirty minutes of intense mental and physical concentration to put the darn contraption together . . . even the wrong way. And another twenty minutes to finally get it together right.

I know some ministers and Bible teachers who twist the Scriptures into doctrines almost as complicated as the directions for assembling that sweater dryer. In seminary I became frustrated to the point of tears trying to read complicated theological texts whose authors were far more concerned with impressing other theologians with their profundity than with helping young preachers understand the Scriptures and the basic principles of the Christian faith. In my classes we spent far more time reading and discussing books *about* the Bible than we spent studying the Word of God itself.

Those frustrating experiences have sometimes prompted me—when asked if I attended seminary—to answer, "Yes, but I finally managed to get over it."

For all the inspirational and self-help books I have read, when I'm having a really difficult time, I find the greatest help and encouragement in the Word of God itself. Maybe that's because what the Scriptures claim for themselves is true.

All scripture is given by inspiration of God, and is profitable for doctrine, for reproof, for correction, for instruction in righteousness: That the man of God may be perfect, thoroughly furnished unto all good works.
                                    2 Timothy 3:16–17, KJV

Their clear simple truths have it all over man's advice, which all too often proves about as helpful as, "Slip single tabbed arm extension into each slotted sleeve with double tabbed bend pointing upward."

— 45

Fumbles
Are Part of the Game

I have a certain weakness that my wife tolerates with gracious resignation: I like to watch professional football on television. During football season our social activities on Sunday afternoons and Monday nights suffer a steep decline since those hours I become "glued to the tube." But even watching football on television, one can learn some helpful lessons about life. Like the game I watched a couple of years ago.

It was one of those games where one team dominates the first half, the other team the second half. Ahead by 21 to 0 at half time, the favored team seemed headed for an easy victory. But suddenly, in the second half, they could do nothing right. Five fumbles recovered by the other side resulted in scores and the favored team lost the game, 35 to 21.

The losing coach was interviewed on TV after the game.

"We hated to lose this one," he admitted. Then he added, *"But fumbles are part of the game."*

The coach's candid observation applies not just to football but to the Christian life as well. I find that generally, Christians fall into two groups: those willing to run the risk of fumbling for a chance to win the victory, and those who play it safe by sitting on the bench. Frankly, I'm convinced that God can do much more with the man who carries the ball knowing he may fumble than with the man who merely watches from the safety of the sidelines.

Fear of failure paralyzes many people. In spiritual counseling, I've listened time and again to timid Christians sharing ambitions, hopes, and dreams they never had the courage to put legs under. For them, fear of fumbling is stronger than the desire for victory.

Yet the Bible is full of heroes who fumbled but went on to finish the game, men and women whom God used in spite of their frailties. Some didn't win, but all of them advanced the Kingdom of God.

David fumbled badly when he took another man's wife and had her husband killed, and his family suffered greatly because of his mistake. Nevertheless, he remained "a man after God's own heart," and eventually found his place in the genealogy of Jesus. In fact, the New Testament refers to Jesus as "the Son of David."

Moses played a great game in leading the children of Israel from bondage in Egypt to the Promised Land, only to fumble by striking the rock God had told him only to speak to. Water came forth just as God promised, but because of his fumble, Moses glimpsed but could not enter the Promised Land (Numbers 20:10–12). A hero of the faith nonetheless, he was lovingly laid to rest in a grave dug by God Himself (see Deuteronomy 34:6).

Peter fumbled when he denied the Lord, Thomas fumbled when he doubted the Resurrection, Paul fumbled when he persecuted the Christians, but all of them finished the game. They kept the faith, they won the victory.

The book of Hebrews lists some faithful heroes who fumbled and "did not receive what was promised" (see chapter 11, verse 39), yet the final victory is theirs as well as ours. Meanwhile, they are securely enshrined in the heavenly hall of fame.

The truth is, everyone who carries the ball fumbles sometime or other. If we may refer to a hero in another sport, Babe Ruth has been immortalized as the "Home Run King." Not so well known is the fact that he also struck out at bat more times than any other major league hitter in his day.

It's no sin to fumble. Failure isn't evil, it's only human, and no life escapes its touch. So the next time you drop the ball at some critical moment, don't despair. Don't be afraid to pick it up and run again. Don't give up and head for the sidelines. Just remember, fumbles are part of the game. And even though the game isn't over, the final outcome is assured. Even though the opposition doesn't want us to believe it, Jesus has already scored the winning touchdown.

And that day will come when He will show us that in His matchless strategy for winning, all our fumbles were taken into account.

"Thanks be to God, who gives us the victory through our Lord Jesus Christ" (1 Corinthians 15:57, NAS).

Follow Me
Only If I Follow Jesus

Follow my example, as I follow the example of Christ.

1 Corinthians 11:1

Most of us have heroes, people whose lives have played a significant role in shaping our own. One of mine was a unique saint named Rufus Moseley. Brother Rufus was a joyous troubadour for the Lord, traveling the country sharing the love of God and testifying to the supreme reality of Jesus Christ. But while a number of men in Christian leadership today were greatly influenced by his life and teaching, Rufus never sought a following. In fact, he worked diligently to avoid a constituency.

In defense of his policy of discouraging followers, he would say, "It's all right to follow me as long as I am following Jesus. But if I go astray, you will too. It's better to be a 'firsthand' follower of Jesus."

The Bible records a number of cases where people got in trouble by blindly following teachers who went astray. When the

Israelites followed the false prophet Balaam, it cost 24,000 of them their lives (see Numbers 25:1–9; 31:16).

Paul chastised the Galatians for following the Judaizers (Jewish teachers known as "the circumcision party") who sought to lead them back into bondage under the law.

> You foolish Galatians! Who has bewitched you? . . . Are you so foolish? After beginning with the Spirit, are you now trying to attain your goal by human effort? . . . Does God give you his Spirit and work miracles among you because you observe the law, or because you believe what you heard?   Galatians 3:1–5

As inspiring as it is to have heroes and as right as it is to honor those who have authority over us and obey them "so that their work will be a joy, not a burden" (see Hebrews 13:17), we should guard against letting our loyalty to any man become a substitute for following the Lord Jesus Himself.

As a leader in the Church, Paul knew he had a responsibility to be a proper example to those he led. "Follow my example," he said. But recognizing his own limitations, he added wisely, "As I follow the example of Christ." The clear implication of Paul's statement was that the Corinthians should *not* follow his example any time he failed to follow Christ. The Church would be a vastly different place if every leader were humble enough to acknowledge his limitations and not expect his followers to follow his mistakes.

After all, God has no perfect people to work through. Thus, every human leader, no matter how talented or efficient, will make mistakes. But if our relationship to those who are leading us is proper, we can learn from their mistakes without having to repeat them. All of which reminds me of the time my brother Hal, a U.S. Air Force major, took our father and me fishing . . . .

Our destination was a river not many miles from the Air Force base in south Texas where Hal was stationed. The river was wide and shallow except for its main channel, which flowed between rocky banks and over an equally rocky bed laced with deep crevices.

We got out of the car, gathered our fishing gear, and stepped to the water's edge. All of us were dressed in khakis and tennis shoes, suitable garb for wading. Since Dad and I were strangers to the river, Hal sounded a note of warning.

"We must get out to the main channel to fish, but it's tricky wading! You can step off into a deep hole very easily. Now, I've fished this river many times, so follow me. I'll show you where the holes are."

And with the confident stride of one who knows the way, Hal stepped into the rushing knee-deep water and headed toward the main channel. Acknowledging the authority experience commands, Dad and I meekly followed in single file. We hadn't gone far when Hal stopped to point at a dark swirl in the water a few feet to his right.

"Deep hole, right there," he called back over his shoulder. "Be careful!" A few steps further on, he stopped and pointed to his left. "And that's another one right there." Dad nodded his head solemnly after each revelation.

"Stay close now," Hal warned, as he took two steps forward again.

"I've traced this route—" And with step number three, he suddenly disappeared. Straight down, out of sight! The rushing water closed over Hal's head, while his fishing hat, covered with his favorite lures, went floating serenely downstream.

Hal bobbed to the surface in front of us, arms flailing.

"—very carefully!" He spouted the final words instinctively. Blowing and sputtering, he struggled to regain his footing in shallower water.

A broad smile split Dad's face. "Another deep hole, son? Thank you for showing it to us! Shall we follow you in or go around?"

Hal glared at us. "Don't move until I get back!" he said, then splashed off across the shallows to retrieve his hat. By the time he returned, the humor of the situation had reached him, and the three of us burst into laughter together.

We went on and caught fish, but today what I remember most about the trip is the lesson I learned about the limitations of leadership. We are to follow those in leadership as long as they are following Christ.

But not *too* closely, since only Jesus knows where *all* the deep holes are.

Still More
Than Conquerors

There is no greater challenge in the Christian life than learning how to live with disappointment, failure, and tragedy. One answer to that challenge (and one of the great redemption secrets of the Christian faith) is found in the familiar verse of Scripture:

And we know that all things work together for good to them that love God, to them who are the called according to his purpose. Romans 8:28, KJV

The man who penned those words—Paul, the apostle—was no stranger to pain and hardship (see 2 Corinthians 11:23–27). Yet his perspective in the midst of cruel circumstances was one of optimistic joy. "In all these things we are more than conquerors through him who loved us" (Romans 8:37).

Failure and even tragedy are as much a part of life as happiness and success. For Christians, when such crises arise, the answer is not found in running away or giving up, but in meeting them with a victorious perspective. If we give in to despair, they will defeat us. But if we face them and say with Paul, "In all these things we are more than conquerors," then events that would otherwise knock us out of the Kingdom serve instead to drive us to the very heart of God.

People who have come through such experiences in victory leave a lasting impact on all our lives. Alice and I met one such couple shortly after we were married. Ed and Ruth Seymour were filled with the joy and confidence that only a tested faith can bring, and Ed's blindness had in no way diminished his effectiveness as a Methodist pastor and Bible teacher. Moreover, he handled his sightlessness so beautifully that people were often around him for hours before discovering he was blind. ("Glad to see you, Alice. You look really lovely tonight.")

Ed's wife, Ruth, had the loveliest clear blue eyes that ever graced a woman's face. "I suppose it's because I must do the seeing for both of us," she often replied to compliments about her eyes.

Twenty-three years before we met them in 1950, Ed and Ruth were a young couple in their first pastorate near Baltimore, facing a future bright with promise, when one Sunday Ed preached a sermon using as his text Romans 8:28. Afterward, a parishioner with severe personal problems confronted him at the door.

"Reverend Seymour, do you really believe that Scripture?"

Ed responded that he did. Then the man grabbed him by the coat lapels and drew his face close.

"But suppose something really bad happened to you? Would you still be able to say, 'All things work together for good to them that love the Lord'?"

Ed felt his second answer come from somewhere deep in his own spirit.

"By the grace of God, I believe I would still be able to say it."

That was on Sunday. The following Tuesday morning while quail hunting with friends, Ed was struck full in the face by a charge of bird shot. Lying on the ground, he raised his hands to his bleeding face and knew he was blind. It was at that moment that Ed heard God's voice speak clearly to him. "You will *still* be able to say that 'all things work together for good.' " Ed's effective ministry stood over the years as eloquent testimony that God had kept His word.

Ed and Ruth Seymour's long and fruitful years of service inspired countless numbers of Christians, including a young man and his wife just beginning their own service to the Lord. Today, thirty-three years after meeting Ed and Ruth, and working in ministry marked by our own share of tragedies and triumphs, heartaches and rich rewards, we add our testimony to theirs: "All things work together for good to them that love God, to them who are called according to His purpose."

P.S. The essay above appeared in *New Wine* magazine in April 1984. I wrote it assuming that Ed Seymour had long since gone on to be with the Lord. After all, he was in his fifties when Alice and I knew him, and an additional thirty-three years had passed.

How surprised and elated I was when just two weeks after it appeared in print, I received a letter from Ed Seymour, still very much alive and serving the Lord, and now residing in a Methodist retirement home not far from Baltimore, the city where he pastored for so many years. Another resident in the retirement home, a subscriber to *New Wine,* opened his April issue and found the article about Ed.

"Hey, Ed," he shouted across the room. "This magazine has an article about you!" Then he read him the article. The same day, Ed sent me a letter, part of which I want to share with you.

Dear Don,
   One of my neighbors regularly receives *New Wine* magazine. Imagine my surprise when he brought me the April issue and

read me page 35, the article in which you reviewed my work in helping build the Kingdom. . . .

Now, after more than fifty years of blindness I still don't look on it as a handicap, but rather as an asset. It has been especially so in my thirty-five years of counseling. I will be 89 my next birthday, this coming July. God has blessed me with good health; I don't feel a day over 70! I can say with St. Paul that by the grace of God, "I am what I am."

My first wife, Ruth, died in 1975 after a long illness. I remarried in 1980, a lovely woman whose family lived within a mile of my family in Baltimore. We both attended the same grade school. We had not seen each other in many years when we met at a religious seminar. We now live in Asbury Village, Gaithersburg, Md., a Methodist retirement center.

Thirty-three years ago, while a minister at Boundary Methodist Church in Baltimore, I established a Saturday breakfast club with twelve dedicated men. The club now has over 125 members. The first Saturday in March there were 102 men present. I will be speaking there again, the first Saturday in June, on the subject, "Let Go and Let God."

I answered Ed's letter immediately and at length, bringing him up-to-date on things like ministry, children, and grandchildren. Later, we had a long telephone conversation in which Ed reported how reading the article had given him a tremendous spiritual lift.

"I guess I was becoming a little discouraged about things, Don," he said. "But it was so encouraging to know that you and Alice remembered me after all these years. And your article in the magazine has given me a spiritual shot in the arm. I've just had twenty-five photocopies of the article made to distribute to Christian friends. I am convinced that there is still much I can do to serve the Lord."

I explained to Ed that one reason we remembered him so well was because Alice and I still read aloud regularly to each other from a dog-eared, badly worn copy of Thomas à Kempis' *The*

Imitation of Christ, a devotional classic, which he and his wife gave us when we first met them back in 1950.

Not many Christians have the privilege of serving the Lord in this life as long as Ed Seymour. After our conversation I found myself praying, "God, should You grant me as many years on earth as You have granted Ed Seymour, let my life be as faithful and fruitful at age eighty-nine as his. Amen."

48

The Best
We Have to Offer

One way our love for the Lord can be measured is by the quality of the gifts we bring to him. I remember a deaconess in a church I pastored years ago coming to me with tears in her eyes. She had been given the responsibility to collect gifts of clothing and other useful articles to be shipped overseas to our missionaries.

"I'm so ashamed of some of the donations," she said. Then I listened in disbelief as she named some of the trashy offerings. Broken tools, ragged linens and patched clothing, worn-out shoes. Even used toothbrushes and half-used tubes of toothpaste.

"How can people be so selfish?" The deaconess shook her head. "It makes me want to weep."

It didn't make me want to weep; it made me furious! (Can you imagine someone actually offering Jesus ragged linen and a used toothbrush?) I went to my study and began preparing a sermon on giving that would have ripped the hide off half of my congregation. But I never got to finish it, much less preach it. Halfway through my preparation I felt as if God spoke silently to me.

"What are you doing?"

"Lord, I intend to rebuke my people for their stinginess!"

"Rebuke *whose* people?"

"Well, *Your* people."

"I see. Is your attitude any better than theirs?"

I quickly saw that God would not approve of my self-righteous rebuking any more than He approved of their self-righteous stinginess.

I felt I also needed to repent for not leading my people—or rather, *His* people—to a level of commitment that would have expressed itself in truly sacrificial giving to our missionaries.

We will never be first-rate Christians as long as we practice second-rate giving. Remember the story in Scripture where Jesus watched the people bringing their offerings to the Temple treasury?

> Many rich people threw in large amounts. But a poor widow came and put in two very small copper coins, worth only a fraction of a penny. Calling his disciples to him, Jesus said, "I tell you the truth, this poor widow has put more into the treasury than all the others. They all gave out of their wealth; but she, out of her poverty, put in everything—*all she had to live on.*"
>
> Mark 12:41–43, italics added

Have you ever wondered why Jesus did not restrain the poor widow's extravagance? How could He just stand there and let her give away everything she had! Why didn't He *do* something? "No, no, little lady! God doesn't want your last penny! Here, take this money!"

I think Jesus did nothing because He knew her extravagant devotion assured that widow a special place in the heart of God. Rufus Moseley once commented about this story in his own inimitable way: "If God wouldn't do all He could for her, after she had done all she could for Him, then better she be God than He be God."

The truth is, we cannot outgive God. Anyone who understands the spiritual laws of sowing and reaping must believe that remarkable widow returned home to find groceries piled high against her front door.

Of course, that's not the reason she gave all she had. She didn't give to get, she gave to show her love. Nevertheless, her extravagant devotion assured her of abundant grace.

And people can be extravagant in other ways to show their love for the Lord. I remember a story describing a great cathedral that was famous for its majestic architecture and superb furnishings. The architects who designed and built it and the artists who painted its murals and carved its ornate interior were men of great renown.

After many years the cathedral roof required major repairs, so scaffolding was erected inside the sanctuary to enable workmen to reach the high, vaulted ceiling. One day, as workmen clambered cautiously among the rafters, high above the cathedral floor where light seldom penetrated, they discovered a magnificent offering left by some unknown artist who intended it for God's eyes alone. There in the gloom, carved in the center of one of the great wooden beams supporting the roof, was an exquisite rendering of the Nativity scene. Inspiring in beauty and seemingly faultless in execution, it surpassed all other works of art in the cathedral.

I can't recall if the story was truth or fiction. But if it was true, then I believe that humble artist must have carried a special secret joy in his heart all the rest of his life, since that kind of giving prompts that kind of reward.

Yet how few of us ever give the Lord the best we have! Too often the only thing we offer the Lord the best of is our excuses. Have you ever given God some lavish gift? Have you ever shown your love for Him in some extravagant way?

Those who have not only find a special secret joy; they are often amazed at what God does in return, just to show His delight.

— 49

Three Grapefruit Halves

And my God shall supply all your needs according to His
riches in glory in Christ Jesus.   Philippians 4:19, NAS

A few years back, I gave several months of intensive study to
the subject of economics, and the more I studied, the more depressed I became. Most modern economists sound like prophets
of doom. Almost all of them agree that, statistically, the world
faces an economic crisis of such mammoth proportions that its
economy will soon collapse and life the way we now live it will be
radically changed.

Their grim statistics include some scary facts: the world's
dwindling natural resources, air and water pollution, our nation's
two-trillion-dollar national debt, a 1986 dollar that bought what
only four cents bought in 1940, borrower nations threatening
default on hundreds of billions of dollars of debt, increasing numbers of bank foreclosures, and various other gloomy statistics.

I became so concerned about those statistics I even gave a
number of Bible teachings on the economic dangers we face and

how our failure to follow biblical principles has led us to the brink of economic disaster.

Then I came to see that quoting scary statistics to prove the crisis exists doesn't really help much. There are already too many experts doing that. What the Christian world needs is *good* news. The bad news is that the world does face an economic crisis of staggering proportions. The good news is that God is still in charge of His world and will always uphold those who love and trust Him.

Most economists leave out what I call the God factor. But His laws have not been revoked, His promises have not failed. There are no shortages in God. He has given us a world where there will always be enough for everyone, *if things are done His way.*

Doomsayer economists describe the wealth of the world as if it were a fixed pie, steadily being cut into increasingly smaller slices with everyone getting less and less. But they fail to take into consideration the creative power of God. They don't realize that the One who spoke the universe into being out of nothing, who blessed and divided a little lad's lunch of five loaves and two fishes into a feast for five thousand men with twelve baskets left over, is still in the business of providing for His own.

I was standing in the kitchen one morning, remembering some of those scary economic statistics and at the same time quietly praising God who delights in meeting our needs. Planning to squeeze some grapefruit juice for Alice and myself, I plugged in the juicer and opened the refrigerator to discover one whole grapefruit plus half of another, wrapped in plastic, left from the day before.

The leftover grapefruit half yielded half a glass of juice, and so did the first half of the whole grapefruit, filling between them one modest-sized glass of juice.

Sliding the full glass to one side, I placed another glass under the juicer and proceeded to squeeze the final half, assuming it would also make only one-half glass of juice and that I would

have to borrow some from the first glass to make them even—
three-fourths of a glass of juice for each of us.

But as I pressed the second grapefruit half against the rotating
juicer, juice just kept flowing until the glass was full. I was
stunned! How could one half of a grapefruit make only one half a
glass of juice and the other half make a whole glass?

Then, remembering why I had just been praising God, I
laughed out loud. To think that a God who miraculously provided 2½ million Israelites wandering in the wilderness with daily
manna for forty years would just as miraculously provide one
Bible teacher standing in his kitchen with an extra half glass of
grapefruit juice for breakfast! I could almost see God smiling,
and almost hear Him saying, "You're right, son, there are no
shortages in Me!"

Some who read this may insist on some natural explanation for
what happened. Perhaps one half of the grapefruit was riper and
had more juice than the other. Or maybe I squeezed the second
half longer and harder than the first half.

Maybe.

But if that's what you must say in order to explain your God's
reluctance to act, I much prefer my God to yours. I choose to go
on trusting in a God who knows His children's needs and is eager
to meet them. Any other God is too small.

— 50

The Communion of Saints

For years I have believed that the curtain separating this life from the next is very thin. Sometimes, for a little while, it almost seems to disappear altogether. The writer of the book of Hebrews may have experienced just such a time when, after recalling the heroes of the faith in Hebrews 11, he goes on to say:

> Thereafter, since we are surrounded by such a great cloud of witnesses, let us throw off everything that hinders and the sin that so easily entangles, and let us run with perseverance the race marked out for us.   Hebrews 12:1

When he spoke of being "surrounded by a great cloud of witnesses," he may have been aware not only of their memory, but of the unseen presence of those heroes themselves, standing just beyond the curtain, not only encouraging him, but encouraging him to encourage us as well.

Now before you jump to the wrong conclusion, let me add that I am probably more aware of the dangers of spiritualism than most Christians. For years I have taught about the evils of occultism, and have even written a book on the subject.[1]

Yet we should never forget that the assurance of personal immortality lies at the heart of our faith and that during certain rare and unexpected moments, and for reasons never clear to us, God allows the curtain between this world and the next to be temporarily drawn aside.

Baseball fans will recall how, in September of 1985, Pete Rose broke the 4,191 base hit record of Ty Cobb, one of baseball's immortals. I watched the TV film of the historic moment. For a few moments, when his teammates rushed onto the field to congratulate him, Pete Rose handled his emotions pretty well. Then suddenly, he broke down and cried. Later, in a TV interview he explained. "I was doing all right, at first," he said. Then he added, *"Until I looked up and saw my father and Ty Cobb."* In his moment of triumph, for Pete Rose—even though he does not profess to be a religious man—the curtain between this world and the next was drawn back.

Two years ago, during the worship service in a small church in Ohio, that same curtain was drawn back for me. At the time I was under some severe personal stress and was battling some rather frightening physical symptoms as well. Perhaps my own spiritual and physical vulnerability at the time may have contributed to what happened, but I'm not sure.

I was sitting in a chair up front, waiting for my time to speak, and we were singing a lovely little chorus whose words included:

> *Commune with me, commune with me;*
> *Between the wings of the cherubim,*
> *Commune with me.*

As we sang those simple words, the whole place was flooded with the presence of God. His love seemed to permeate the room

[1] *The Most Dangerous Game*, Fleming H. Revell, Old Tappan, N.J., 1974.

with a sweetness unlike anything I had ever experienced. It was as if some secret doorway to heaven had swung open and we were breathing another, more holy atmosphere.

Then all at once, I was aware that saints from that other realm were joining our worship. Among those I sensed, but never saw, were the spirits of my father and three other godly men: Rufus Moseley, the saintly Bible teacher and spiritual troubadour; Dr. Frank Laubach, a world-renowned missionary and literacy expert; and Dr. G. Edwin Osborn, a gentle seminary professor and friend. I had known all of them personally, and each one had greatly influenced my life and ministry. Don't ask me *how* I knew they were there, they were just there, joining in worship more precious than any we had ever enjoyed together on earth, sharing a fellowship so sacred I scarcely dared to breathe. It was an experience I shall never forget.

There were no words, no messages, no revelations, only the quiet and serene presence of godly men who had finished the race and who seemed to want to assure me—from their higher vantage point—that all was well.

Before beginning my message, for a soggy five minutes I tried to explain what had happened to me. Tearful nods from the minister and from some in the audience suggested I was not the only one who had sensed the presence of unseen loved ones.

I don't remember what I spoke about that day. Whatever the message, it was strictly anticlimactic.

I left that little church filled with a fresh assurance that no matter how difficult our current trials or how great our present problems and temptations, the future for everyone who loves the Lord Jesus is more than just bright; it is wonderfully, eternally secure. Moreover, it is a future that holds in store for each of us a reunion more joyful than any we can presently imagine.